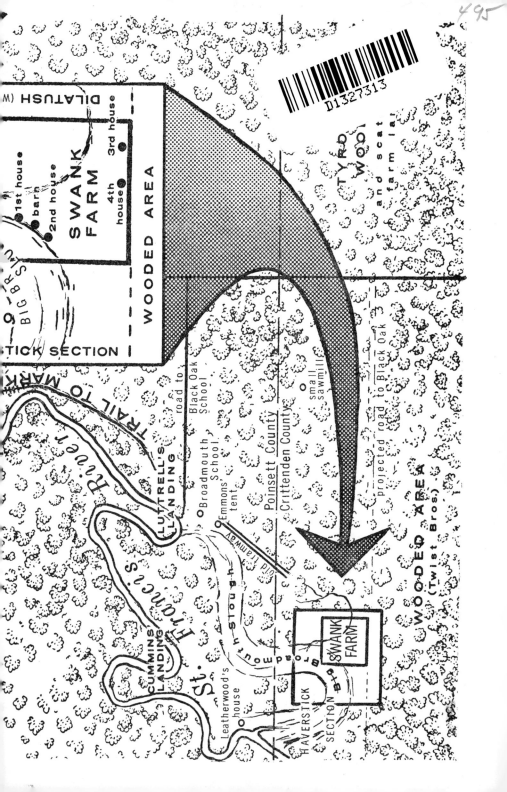

TRAIL TO MARKED TREE

TRAIL
TO
MARKED
TREE

BY ROY SWANK

Edited with an Introduction
by Nolan Porterfield

The Naylor Company
Book Publishers of the Southwest
San Antonio, Texas

Each plant that fluted up in long rows
out of the soil was native to its
particular few inches of rootage, and held
relationship among these others to the work and
living of some particular man and family,
in a particular house, perhaps whose lamp I
saw beneath this field; and each tree
had now its own particular existence and
personality, stood up branching
out of its special space in the spreading of
its blood, and stayed there waiting,
a marked man, a tree:

— JAMES AGEE
Let Us Now Praise Famous Men

"Dizzily they crossed the river: at night he saw the small
bleared shacks of Arkansas set in malarial fields."

— THOMAS WOLFE
Look Homeward, Angel

PREFACE

This is a personal narrative of early twentieth century life in the wooded delta lowlands of northeast Arkansas. It focuses upon the events of about six years, from 1919 to 1926, a moment in history now almost half a century old.

I have made no attempt to produce a work of profound research, but have intended simply to give an account of the backwoods pioneering experiences of my brother and myself. My aim is to present a realistic picture of everyday living in the hinterlands. Certainly it is a bit of Americana that has been neglected.

Possibly I am one of the few remaining pioneers of that area or time who might be able to give expression to the mood and way of living in that shrouded, earlier day. I can, of course, write more freely now than would have been possible forty years ago. The subject can be handled with more objectivity and with greater frankness than would have been permissible then.

Although it was not a country "where the foot of man never trod and the eye of man never saw," we were deep inside a woods of over eight thousand acres, linked to "civilization" by only a few rudimentary roadways and turbulent, undependable rivers. We were more isolated than many of the first explorers and settlers, more enmeshed and entangled in the woods and woodland ways than was Thoreau at Walden Pond seventy-five years earlier. And because we were so fully a part of the region for an extended period, we had a unique opportunity to observe and jot down — mostly in letters — details of the little-known conditions of people in the Arkansas lowlands — the way they lived, worked, hunted, traveled, fought, and sometimes died. We saw them cutting away the timberlands, toiling over scrubby cotton crops, building homes, fighting flood waters, making moonshine, laughing, mourning, trying to make things better for themselves and their families. It was a country where privations and common needs bound people more closely together and inured them to hardship. Its people and its way of life are, it seems to me, all too frequently unknown or misunderstood by outsiders.

Here I echo the words of Robert Burns who, in his diary for October 1785, warned that if anyone "chances to throw his eye over these pages, let him pay warm attention to the following observations, as I assure him they are the forests of a poor fellow's dear-bought experience." Perhaps Burns' metaphor has special meaning for those of us who cleared timberland and put it to plow, who remember the comfortable weariness that followed a day on the business end of a crosscut saw or double-bit forester's axe.

Although I have drawn on my own intimate memories in collecting this material, this book would have been quite impossible without the many letters which my brother Will and I wrote home to Ohio during our years of roughing it in Arkansas. Also vital were those letters to Edna Wilson, now my wife. Practically every letter was faithfully preserved, thanks to the recipients, and they furnished a rich treasury of firsthand news and observations. We seem to have been loyal correspondents and accurate chroniclers. My brother (now deceased) was further qualified by his earlier experience as a newspaper reporter, which had given him an observant eye and a fluency of expression, in addition to his natural flair for writing. Also, a number of others have contributed in various ways to this memoir. It would be difficult to acknowledge all my indebtedness, but first of course is the special gratitude I owe Nolan Porterfield, of The University of Iowa, whose interest, encouragement, and advice have been invaluable. Working with me faithfully in editing the manuscript and preparing it for publication, even to the extent of visiting Marked Tree to fill in details and record fresh impressions, he has offered innumerable suggestions and seen to it that I eventually said all the things I should have said in the first place. Many of the comments he jotted into the manuscript I have

viii

preserved without change; any errors, however, are of my own origin.

I am also deeply indebted to Mrs. Grace Ryder, teacher of English at Newark, Ohio, High School; to Miss Alda Fowler, of Chester, West Virginia, who taught English for over thirty years in the East Liverpool, Ohio, High School; and to my wife, Edna, for their thorough work in going over the manuscript; and to Miss Betty Fulke, who assisted in its preparation. Dr. H. O. Grauel, Chairman of the English Department at Southeast Missouri State College, also gave willingly of his time and knowledge; I am grateful for the opportunity to thank him.

Further, my sincere thanks to my niece, Mrs. Bill (Bob-bye) Jones of Lexington, Kentucky; and my brother's widow, Mrs. Gladys Swank Bridger of Marked Tree, both of whom helped in numerous ways and gave me advice and encouragement. I should also like to record the contribution of my good friend Harold Hughes of Newark, who throughout the days of his last illness was an able and patient advisor to this project, the completion of which he did not live to see.

Roy Swank
Newark, Ohio

CONTENTS

	Introduction	xiii
I	THE LAND OF BEGINNING AGAIN: An Amateur Historian Reflects on Frontiers, Childhoods, and Airplanes	1
II	FORWARD INTO THE PAST: Railroad Tracks Turn to Timber Trails	14
III	A LODGE IN THE WILDERNESS: Home, Home on the Slough	20
IV	WOUNDS OF MEN AND OF TREES: We Find a New Friend, Clear the Land, and Endure a Disaster	30
V	PLOWING NEW GROUND: Old Roots Are Torn Up, New Ones Put Down	37
VI	COTTON AND 'CROPPERS: A Saga of People Against "A Bug Long Years Ago"	44
VII	BOOTS AND BOATS: Some Observations That Are All Wet	56
VIII	THE TREES FELL: View From One End of a Crosscut Saw	65
IX	MAN AND BEAST: Wildlife in "All Righten Country"	74
X	SNAKES AND MOSQUITOES: The Venomed Stings of Life — and Death	89
XI	MOONSHINE AND MAYHEM: The Extra-Strength Pain Relievers	102
XII	THE PASSING PARADE: Fun and Games	116
XIII	FIRES OF TRIBULATION: The Rains Came, the Earth Trembled, and the Flames Raged	133
XIV	GOLDEN RULE DAYS: Tenting on the Old Schoolground	140
XV	THE TRAIL ENDS: Of Time, the River, and the Men	156

INTRODUCTION

A sense of the past is a fine and terrible thing.

It is a singularly human affliction, suffered only by those intelligently irrational enough to ask such simple but impossible questions as "Who am I?" and "Where did I come from?"

Moreover, it seems to be a disease peculiar to modern man, striking with greater frequency and intensity as civilization advances and the future bears down on the present with increasing velocity.

Thus we observe the space-age paradox of man rocketing out toward the new worlds of tomorrow while at the same time digging, literally and figuratively, back into the yesterdays of this old one, in an ever-expanding, almost obsessive quest to recapture the past, as demonstrated not only in the proliferation of scholarly history, but in the current mania for antiquity of all forms, among scholars and amateurs alike. The nation teems with Civil War buffs, weekend archeologists, commemorative societies, and collectors of every old thing from coins to fluting irons and barbed wire.

The pursuit of history has already taken man far beyond his first motives. That is the beautiful part of it — that he can go out looking for "Who am I?" and come back laden with lost Bible scrolls, a more accurate date for the beginnings of American civilization, the source for one of Shakespeare's plays, the forgotten diary of a great statesman, the exposure of a dozen specious myths from The Good Old Days, the truth about Lincoln's early life, a detailed reconstruction of Custer's final march to the Little Bighorn, countless spoils of time uncharted on any treasure map of mind or soul.

Yet all too often the elementary questions remain unanswered, and the seeker of the past, surrounded by his many documents and charts and relics, stares wonderingly at a faded tintype or a chip of flint, and he wonders on:

xiii

What was it *really* like with them? How did the land lay then, and who first walked across it? What were the smells and where did the shadows reach and when did it all change? As this was being made and that done and something else planned, what were they thinking and saying and feeling? To such questions the history books and Hollywood's period epics and the fake time machines of television are silent, and for those of us with a sense of the past, the silence is terrible.

Happily, Roy Swank has written a book that is full of sound. *Trail to Marked Tree* answers with skill and moving vigor the important questions about a particular time and place, where, in the author's words, there were "few comforts, little money, and nowhere to spend it; cattle, but no fences; wagons, and no roads; few laws, and even fewer people to administer them; plenty of outlaws, preachers, and patent medicine peddlers, but not many doctors, teachers, or philosophers; a sparse population that was self-reliant, interdependent, and tough as a tempered wagon tire." Perhaps this history succeeds so well merely because its author writes as a man with a feeling for time and people, rather than as a formal historian. Whatever the reason, his remembrances of things past, as represented here, are a lively testament to the truth of Bertrand Russell's observation that "as soon as you know the general outline of history of some period, it becomes agreeable and profitable to read the letters and memoirs of the time, [for] they contain much intimate detail which makes it possible to realize that the men concerned really lived."

Reading the manuscript of *Trail to Marked Tree* was immediately "agreeable and profitable" to me. There was no doubt in my mind that the "men concerned" really lived, for Mr. Swank makes them live again, vividly and genuinely. It speaks a great deal for his book that I was, in fact, so caught up with the force of the narrative that I went to see for myself where it all happened — the muddy St. Francis, Broadmouth Slough, the slumbering remains of

Marked Tree. Certainly not every reader will be so moved, and I hasten to add that there were private and subjective reasons for such interest: my own peculiar sense of the past, a special attraction to the 1920's and 30's, the time of which Mr. Swank writes, and finally the coincidence that his odyssey to Arkansas paralleled in so many ways the pioneering experiences of my own grandfather on the bleak plains of West Texas at about the same time.

I was also struck by the way in which Mr. Swank's view of the "bypassed and forgotten frontiers" of this century fitted into the pattern of family history as I had observed it. My great-grandfather had been among those who, in the great westward migration, touched briefly in Arkansas before moving on, at the turn of the century, into northern Texas. The leap-frog game was resumed a generation later, when my grandfather traveled West in a caravan of T-Model and wagon, leaving behind civilization, erosion, and the boll weevil to homestead on the Staked Plains, where the land had been broken but never settled. As Mr. Swank observes, Frederick Jackson Turner to the contrary, it was not until the next generation, in my father's time, that men — those who worked the soil, at least — finally stopped looking west.

To be sure, pioneering was not the same in West Texas as in the Arkansas Delta. The most obvious difference involved trees and water: while my grandfather fought sandstorms and drought, Mr. Swank was floating log rafts and heading for high ground to escape floods. But cotton made their lives more alike than different; as the primary crop in both areas, it dominated every aspect of the early settler's life, from the way he shaped his land and built his buildings, to his opinions about God, government, and the goosenecked hoe.

These are things that Roy Swank has recalled for us in *Trail to Marked Tree*: the sad and funny ballads of Big Cooper; Frank Walters and his "tard" mule; Mr. Keth, the man Huckleberry Finn grew up to be; goats in the basement and flies in the ointment; a child's dying; a lover's laugh; a man's burdens; moonshine, sharecroppers, river boats, murders, fires, floods . . . and a little girl who wrote, "I love you. If you will not get mad at me anymore." This is a book not just about human beings, but about what it means to be human, in a unique time and place. Especially appealing is the flavor with which this gently moving epic is related. *Trail to Marked Tree* is a poigant study of a time so near and yet far distant, a time when, as Mr. Swank puts it, "the houses were farther apart and the people closer together." The houses and their inhabitants have multiplied, but the people and the place he writes of no longer exist.

The study of history, like most other disciplines, is from time to time subjected to various fads and dogmas. In recent decades, a large segment of the public has come to cherish the old saw, attributed I believe to Santayana, to the effect that those who ignore history are doomed to repeat it. This dictum has been particularly popular among intense schoolboys, lovers of cliches, and especially, it seems, those who know very little history. It is a fine rule when one has in mind such things as Hitler, prohibition, the Triangle Shirtwaist Fire, child labor, and McCarthyism; but it also implies that we should forego all hope of resurrecting Normalcy, the drugstore soda fountain, big band jazz, Fourth of July picnics, dime novels, nickel beer, penny candy, steam locomotives, the New Deal, the free lunch, the five-cent cigar, and a way of life unharried by time clocks, smog, freeway traffic, and deodorant commercials. The notion that history repeats itself is probably folklore, but if indeed it does, we must force ourselves to take the good along with the bad, as Roy Swank has done, with rare and delicate balance, in the following pages.

NOLAN PORTERFIELD

1 THE LAND OF BEGINNING AGAIN:

An Amateur Historian Reflects on Frontiers, Childhoods, and Airplanes

According to the famous historian, Frederick Jackson Turner, the American frontier disappeared about 1890. To be sure, things by that time had changed a great deal. Cattle drives and wagon trains belonged to the past, along with buffalo herds, Indian wars, the open range, and undiscouraging words. But what concerned Mr. Turner, of course, was the idea that the "continually expanding frontier," as he called it, had been responsible for molding the American character. Moving westward, riding Conestogas, fighting Indians and each other, hacking down virgin forests, polluting rivers, jumping claims, and floating watered rail stock had made us all rugged individualists — tough, resourceful, and most of all, democratic (but not necessarily Democratic). Now that it was all gone, said Mr. Turner, we were in danger of turning into sissies.

1

Maybe so. But I'm inclined to feel that Turner's elegy for the frontier was, like the report of Mark Twain's death, greatly exaggerated. Premature, at least.

Perhaps you've seen a concrete floor or sidewalk being poured. After they dump the raw, wet cement, a couple of fellows lay a long, thick board across the top of the forms, then one gets on each end and they start wiggle-waggling the board over the surface, pushing the gobby cement ahead, leveling it down and forcing it into all the corners. The leveling board leaves some lumps and raw spots behind it, but after a while some more fellows come along with trowels and finish it up all nice and smooth. Figuratively speaking, the West was settled the same way.

After the Civil War, there was a big stampede westward across the continent, a stampede that largely ended when barbed wire closed off the open range and somebody out in California decided it was time to open a subdivision, build a freeway, and put up a Dari-King stand.

But in their quest for greener pastures, the first pioneers, like the leveling board, left rough spots along the way. Many remote or seemingly undesirable areas in the Mid-South and Southwest remained almost untouched, waiting for another generation to come along and smooth out the lumps, cover the cracks and trim the edges. In some of these by-passed and forgotten frontiers, as in northeast Arkansas, the land had been settled briefly, stripped of its timber and other resources, then deserted by its footloose, adventuresome former inhabitants and left to grow back into wilderness. Almost thirty years after Turner's historic pronouncement, I was a pioneer in such a hidden frontier. It had all the earmarks of a genuine, pre-1890 outpost of progress: isolation, privation, violence, ignorance, sickness and vice; few comforts, little money, and nowhere to spend it; cattle but no fences, wagons and no roads; few laws and even fewer people to administer them; plenty of outlaws, preachers, and patent-medicine peddlers, but not many doctors, teachers, or philosophers; a sparse population that was

2

self-reliant, interdependent, and tough as a tempered wagon tire.

In general, this area was the upper delta region of northeast Arkansas — the wooded lowlands between the Mississippi and St. Francis Rivers. Specifically, it was 160 acres about nine miles south of Marked Tree, Arkansas, near the east bank of the St. Francis. When my brother and I went there in 1919, the country was as wild and untamed as it must have been when the first settlers began to appear in the region forty or fifty years earlier.

Not many had come, and even fewer stayed. There had been some profit in logging the timber, but it was hard work and best suited to wildcatters who rented or leased an area, cut the prime growth of timber, and moved on. Farming the land meant, in addition, the tedious, exhausting labor of breaking out the stump-cluttered, root-infested ground. Floods, malaria, and the general remoteness of the area made permanent settlement even less attractive so long as better land was available further west. It was not until the twentieth century was well along in its second decade that the development of this region began in earnest.

The circumstances of my own exodus to Arkansas were a curious blend of the sublime and the ridiculous, the old and the new, the modern and the primitive. For example, the airplane, herald of a new age, was largely, if symbolically, responsible for it all, as I shall explain; and when I set out from my native Ohio on the trail to Marked Tree I traveled not by horse or by prairie schooner but in the relative comfort of a railroad coach (perhaps "an Iron Horse" would sound sufficiently evocative of the frontier).

Once I reached my destination, however, I was immediately struck with the sense of having lost fifty years or so somewhere along the way. Marked Tree in 1919 was a budding city of some 1,500 citizens, but having slumbered through most of the years since its establishment in the early 1880's, the town still bore a close resemblance to one of those frontier outposts in a William S. Hart movie,

3

complete with false fronts, wooden sidewalks, and cattle roaming the unpaved streets. Houses and stores were built up on stilts or high wooden blocks as a defensive measure against frequent floods. The primitive character of the town, however, was nothing compared to what we were to encounter in our attempts to carve out a farm in the wilderness beyond. There, the "trail to Marked Tree" became a fact.

We were pioneers in the original sense of the word — foot soldiers (with great emphasis on the adjective) who, as Webster has it, "go before, laying the way for others to follow, digging, building roads, bridging, preparing the land." Until we built them, there were no roads — and for that matter, few automobiles to run on them. There were no bridges, no improvements of any kind, to say nothing of houses or outbuildings. As for preparing the land — well, we went there to farm, but first the land had to be cleared, and that involved a dozen kinds of "digging, building, bridging and preparing." All this was done without any of the technological advances we take for granted today. We had no power machinery or do-it-yourself kits — no bottled gas, automatic appliances, canned heat, frozen dinners, or instant foods. Our work was done with only the crudest implements . . . largely hand tools and elbow grease. There was no electricity, of course, and nothing much — animal, mineral, or vegetable — to electrify. Mules were the only "power tools" we knew of in those days.

To understand the significance of this, remember that although such conditions had been common fifty or a hundred years before, we were experiencing them far into the twentieth century — after the Great World War; after the introduction of the automobile, the incandescent light, the telephone, the phonograph, movies, radio; after men had Saved The World For Democracy and women began to vote, smoke, and wear slacks. (In June, 1919, shortly before I left for Arkansas, the first trans-Atlantic flight was made — eight years ahead of Lindbergh — by Sir John William

4

Alcock and Lt. Arthur Brown, flying from Newfoundland to Ireland.)

There is double irony in the fact that we were less than forty miles from one of the South's largest cities — Memphis — and hardly twenty years from the Atomic Age. But it seemed like four hundred miles to Memphis, and the atom's only business back then was to reassure us that it was the smallest particle of matter — forever indivisible.

I never fully appreciated the virtues of hardship in Arkansas, but I had been prepared for it by my childhood and upbringing in rural Ohio, which, although quite civilized by comparison, was in the best traditions of the American frontier.

The hill country of southeastern Ohio was my homeland — Muskingum County, of which Zanesville is the county seat. At Zanesville, spanning both the Licking River and the Muskingum, is one of the very few Y-bridges in the world. It and the city's ex-dentist author of western novels constitute Zanesville's chief claim to fame. Zane Grey was, of course, a descendant of Ebenezer Zane, who with John McIntire laid out in 1799 the town whose name still indicates that it is "Zane's town." The famous old Cumberland Road crosses the Muskingum at this point, and the town once served as Ohio's capitol.

The region was originally a land of timbered hills and unbroken forests, but it was settled and cleared so long ago that even in my father's time no traces of stumps remained in cultivated fields. Many farm homes in the area date back to the early years of the nineteenth century. Still standing is the house where I was born in 1891; no one knows exactly when it was built, but it was also the birthplace of my father in 1866, and may have been that of my grandfather in 1804. At any rate, the old house, eight comfortable rooms set on a high hill, has borne the footsteps of several generations.

In my childhood we were "far from the madding crowd," tucked into the hills, surrounded by pastures and corn

5

lands and wheat fields and green forests, with the nearest hamlet four miles away (which in those days was 21,120 feet, or perhaps half that many steps — not four clicks on an auto's odometer). The landscape would serve (and may well have) as a model for one of those scenes of typical America by Stevan Dohanos that used to appear on *Saturday Evening Post* covers a few years back.

By the standards of that time, our family was relatively small — only five children. I was oldest, then came Will, a year and a half younger, followed by Gertrude, born in 1894. The next, Clarence, was ten years younger than Gertrude, and the "baby" of the family, Florence, was born in 1908.

It was a wonderful time and place to grow up, there in the ripe spawning hills of mid-America around the turn of the century. If our life was austere and sometimes harsh, it was also in many ways idyllic. Of course, my memories of it are somewhat colored by the rose-tinted lenses of that built-in rearview mirror through which we humans usually view the past; I look back now with a certain warmth and lightness, on even the most dire calamities that befell us — such as the time Will and I struggled before a gathering storm to herd our cattle into the barn, only to have lightning strike and set it afire moments later. We hurriedly drove the cows back out, and even managed to save some harness and other equipment, which we tossed against a strawpile near the flaming barn. The strawpile promptly caught fire and burned everything we'd salvaged, as well as a chicken house nearby.

I'm always a little suspicious of people who prattle about "the good old days," and no one is more thankful than I am for modern conveniences and the many advances in health, education and social welfare that have been made in recent years. Maybe the nineties *were* gay and the twenties roaring, but nobody in his right mind really wants to go back to the drudgery, disease, and drabness of those times. Yet there was a certain order, a substance to our life

6

back in Ohio. "Guaranteed annual wage" is perhaps an eloquent phrase and an even more eloquent idea, but for us there was no such thing — no government subsidies, no minimum wage laws (and very little wages), no Social Security, no guarantees of any kind, except that life is real and earnest, and tomorrow was coming. The future was up to us. In our particular case, I think the knowledge of this produced the most vital meaning our lives could have had: in responding to it we found the proof and the justification of our being. Man is more than the object of wage laws, the subject of learned tracts, the adverb of time's passing.

The things I remember most clearly from childhood days are those which testify to our self-sufficiency: butchering hogs and smoking the meat; churning cream and counting the strokes of the dasher until it could be rested on the surface as evidence that butter had come; my father riveting harness or sculpting a wagon's singletree from a slab of white oak with axe and draw-knife, or forming sled runners from hickory saplings. In our own fanning mill we recleaned the oats, wheat, and timothy seed we grew. Mother made and mended most of our clothes, washed them in a hand machine ordered from Sears-Roebuck, ironed them with flat-irons heated on the back of the big coal- and wood-burning kitchen range. Pre-prepared foods were unheard of; potatoes, tomatoes, corn, peas and beans came from Mother's garden rather than a grocer's shelves. Our "store-bought" foodstuffs were largely limited to salt, sugar, rice, and, once each season, a keg of Lake Erie herring (the only meat we ever bought).

Such self-sufficiency created an almost mystic relationship with the basic elements of living, a relationship that does not seem to exist today. A thermostat is a dandy thing, of course, but not nearly so satisfying to a child snug abed on a cold winter's morn as his father stirring up — as mine used to do — the slack coal which had covered the fire in the grate overnight. I can still call back the feel of that first warming blaze . . . then the weak but mellow glow of a coal oil lamp, and the heady aroma of pancakes and oatmeal and ham-and-eggs which Mother was "hurrying up." With at least our "innards" warmed, we braved the elements to feed and milk the cows, then returned to pour the rich, creamy "cow juice" through our old De Laval separator, an unknown quantity in most farm homes today.

Our summers were given over to that old Cervantean admonition about making hay while the sun shines. We also "made" corn, oats, and barley, as well as various other things from time to time, including callouses and strong backs. We did not make much mischief, for there was rarely time for it in our busy schedules. By daybreak on most summer mornings, my brother Will and I were on our way, barefooted, into the pasture that stretched away a half mile or more from our barn. There we rounded up the field horses and drove them to the barn, where they were fed and harnessed. Before the sun had completely risen we were in the fields, plowing, planting, cultivating, hoeing. Today, bosses have trouble with clock watchers. My father complained that we were sun watchers. When Sol was straight overhead, it was dinnertime; when he had passed from sight beyond the western hills, it was time to quit. The eight-hour day, alas, had not been invented.

All summer long we prepared for winter; and when winter came, our work went right on. Cows still had to be milked, livestock fed, and stables cleaned. It seemed there was always corn to be husked. We sometimes hauled shucks inside the barn in advance of cold weather so we could go on with husking even when the wind and snow raged outside. But our winter work wasn't always so protected — we often hauled corn fodder from the field in near-blizzard conditions to provide feed for the sheep, cattle, and horses.

I think it was the womenfolks who suffered most from our kind of life, and yet they seemed to bear it best. An incident concerning my mother reveals the spirit they possessed. Mother was having trouble with her teeth. One day when the pain became too much, she simply got into

8

the buggy and went bouncing and rattling all the way to Coshocton, twelve miles distant, up hill and down, over dirt roads. It took her almost four hours to get there. The dentist pulled sixteen teeth, Mother spat, got back into the buggy, and came home — all in the same day. I don't remember exactly, but she probably fixed supper for the family that evening. *This* was the sort of thing that won the West. I'll bet that Kit Carson, Buffalo Bill, and Wyatt Earp were sissies by comparison.

Life was not always so hard, of course. There were various diversions, however tame by today's standards, that afforded relief from the tedium of daily life. I rather like what Thad Snow, Missouri's "Cottonfield Confucius," wrote about his youth in Indiana at a similar time: "There were no movies then or comic books, so we never had a dull moment." For us, Saturday was the high point of the week; that was "butter and egg day," when we took our dairy products to market and exchanged them for the few essentials we did not raise ourselves — plus the bonus of a pound of hard candy, worth ten cents, but usually presented as a gift to us children by the generous grocer.

Our Methodist Church sponsored a picnic in the summertime and a revival during the winter. The latter was often quite an event, and when it snowed we went to church by horse-sled (actually a wagon bed fitted on runners and filled with straw — a far more glamorous mode of transportation than the family auto!). Extra-curricular activities at school were usually limited to a pie social each year, but even such hum-drum affairs had their moments. I remember one occasion when a young lady refused to eat her pie with the fellow who bought it. She suspected him of having partaken of the cup that cheers. Her suspicions were confirmed when he picked up the pie, went outside, and threw it with all his might against the front of the building. (Maybe he knew something too; the pie stuck tight to the wall, and remained pasted there for weeks, despite the efforts of man and nature to remove it.)

9

But our social life, such as it was, was always subordinate to the business of making our living. Once Will and I looked forward to a Fourth of July celebration, which was to us as teenagers in those days roughly the equivalent of a James Bond double feature, with free access to the popcorn and candy stand. For weeks we anxiously awaited the Great Day — which, when it arrived, was so sunny and rare that Dad decided it must not be wasted. Will and I spent that Independence Day (!) building a haystack, as Dad pitched up the hay to us. I've not been quite the same since.

For the most part we took such things in stride. But we never quite conquered or learned to live with the one element that really made our struggles so difficult — those rocky, lurching Ohio hills. We could rid the fields of stones, but the hills were everlasting. Uphill roads often had "breakers" cut across them where horses could rest on tiresome climbs, but there were no breaks or let-ups for us in the tilting fields. It is a vile and wondrous thing to push a plow forward, down, and up — forward in the furrow, down in the ground, and up a hill — all at the same time. Binders toppled on their sides not infrequently, and we harvested oats with cradles where no binder ever dared venture.

During the summers, we children often visited our cousins, the Littles, who lived and farmed a few miles away in the relatively level bottom land of the Muskingum River. There we helped with corn hoeing and marveled that the cornfield had no lower side to be filled in with dirt to support the corn stalks. We were accustomed to the dangers of "falling out of the cornfield," as the old wheeze has it. Working with the Littles was a rare treat, although it had the disadvantage of making our hill work seem much more burdensome by comparison.

The absence of stones along the river bottom was a special delight to me, for I hated the confines of shoeleather and went barefooted until late in my teens (as a matter of choice rather than necessity).

10

In 1907 the family moved to Dresden, about nine miles from our farm home, so that Will and I could attend high school. Scarcely fifty pupils were enrolled in the high school classes, which were conducted in two rooms on the second floor of Dresden's only school building and presided over by the huge, awesome superintendent, Professor Smock and a fretful spinster aptly named Ida Warden. Among our classmates was Bland Stradley, a mischievous lad with a mop of unruly red hair that he always parted in the middle. Bland — as Dr. Stradley — later distinguished himself as a long-time vice-president of Ohio State University.

Interscholastic sports were unknown at Dresden High until about 1908, when a local preacher agreed to try his hand as football coach. His ignorance of the game was surpassed only by that of the members of his team, most of whom had never seen a football.

Nevertheless, we worked hard at it, and soon whipped up a squad that showed real spirit. So intense was our fervor, in fact, that we scheduled our first game against Coshocton, a school several times the size of Dresden. Organized sports were a tradition there, and the game was to be played on Coshocton's home field, but we remained undaunted by such odds. Here was David come to slay Goliath, and to be sure, it was a massacre. Final score 141 to 0 — in favor of Coshocton. We had suffered the worst defeat in the history of Ohio football and perhaps established a national record for all time. Our team scarcely knew enough to bend over in scrimmage.

One of our players, the smallest and greenest (but ultimately the wisest) had taken a look at the situation and decided to elope with his girl instead of playing in the game. Newspapers over the country had great fun with that. "Cupid Defeats Team," read one headline; another boldly, but a bit erroneously, announced, "Star Player Elopes; Team Loses 141 to 0." Perhaps it is unnecessary to add that our first game was also our last.

After graduating in 1910, Will and I attended Mt.

Union College in Alliance, Ohio. Then Will dropped out to work as a newspaper reporter, and I went to Ohio State, where I could specialize in agriculture. Later I transferred to Michigan State at East Lansing and in 1916 got my degree there. After college I taught in high school for a year at Frazeysburg, Ohio, a town not far from where I grew up. Another teacher at Frazeysburg was Miss Edna Wilson, who plays a significant role in the later years of my narrative. In 1918 I went back to my father's farm and for the next year and a half, helped him with the work there.

Meanwhile, with the outbreak of World War I, Will had joined the Army Air Corps. After ground school at Columbus, he was sent to Park Field, near Memphis, Tennessee, for pilot training. There he frequently made cross-country flights to adjoining states where, in various places, temporary landing fields had been constructed. One of these was at Marked Tree, Arkansas.

Here the lush delta country, with its thousands of acres of fine, level cotton land, looked especially inviting to my brother, remembering his boyhood spent in hard farm work in the rough, stony hills of southeastern Ohio. He wrote home glowingly of this marvelous Eden he had discovered. And so it was that an agent of the dawning Air Age became the instrument of our retrogression into the living ways of the past.

From somewhere out of the cool mists of childhood, I recall scattered lines from a wistful little poem about the Land of Beginning Again, "where all our mistakes and all our heartaches are banished forever or slain." I've given up the search for such a place in this world. If it exists at all, it is in our minds, in the way that we gradually learn to live with our mistakes and heartaches. Perhaps it is only in looking back that we see how "the pain of living and the drug of dreams" — to use the words of T. S. Eliot — have, in fact, given our life its fullest meaning.

But back in 1919, mindful only of the few troubles and heartaches I'd already suffered and oblivious to the thou-

12

sands more that were yet to come, I was primed and ready for a Land of Beginning Again. I had always been fascinated by geography — the siren call of strange names and faraway places that torments every schoolboy — and the open road continued to beckon as I grew up. Once I even harbored a yen to live in Madagascar, of all places. But I was committed by training and temperament to farming, and for that the land ought to be "level as a billiard table" — whatever a billiard table might be. Remembering how as a child I'd envied the Littles their flat land in the tiny Muskingum Valley, I hardly dared imagine the splendor of the rich Mississippi Delta, with its fertile alluvial soil and broad acres of cotton. When Will suggested that I come and see for myself, I lost little time in setting out on what was, ultimately, the trail to Marked Tree.

11 FORWARD INTO THE PAST:

Railroad Tracks Turn to Timber Trails

In August, 1919, I was on my way west to St. Louis, then after a change of trains, southward along the banks of the Big Muddy. The war had been over almost a year, but returning troops still marched in victory parades, and Wilson had come home from Versailles to fight his losing battle for the League of Nations. It was the eve of the Jazz Age — bathtub gin, flagpole sitters, flappers, the Charleston, Mah-Jongg, and gang warfare. But little of this touched the world I was entering; the twentieth century seemed to recede into the hills behind me, as if the train were some kind of Wellsian time-machine.

The trip was not uneventful. At some small tank-town in Missouri the train stopped. I got out and crossed the tracks to a little eating place. Before I could finish my snack, the train began to pull out. I rushed out and grabbed a handhold between coaches, but the grillwork was closed on that side. A woman just inside the coach watched my plight but made no effort to help. I tried to make her understand by my motions that I wanted in, but she couldn't seem to comprehend the situation at all, being even dumber than I was. After a minute or two the conductor came along and added his insult. "Trying to lose your train?" he growled. I hung on for dear life. Finally satisfied that I'd suffered enough, he let me in.

Traveling through Missouri, I noticed for the first time a number of Negro passengers in the coach — then suddenly I was surrounded by them, with not another white person in sight. Ignorant of the reason but faintly aware that I didn't belong there, I headed for another coach, where I found only fair skins. Later I learned that we had crossed the state line; Arkansas had a Jim Crow law, while Missouri did not.

I don't recall that there was any gala celebration upon my arrival in Marked Tree. I was met at the station by Brother Will and several stray cows that happened to be roaming by. Will was living at the Gamble Rooming and Boarding House, which we reached by a desultory walk of some two blocks over a wooden sidewalk built up about two feet off the ground (a precaution against floods). The dowdy village of Marked Tree was hardly an auspicious sight, but I was impressed by one thing — it was August and the schools were in session. I thought, how much more education these youngsters must receive than ours in Ohio! I soon learned my mistake. In a few weeks the schools closed until January so that the children could help with the cotton harvest. Then they would resume again for four months or so, until time for planting. The "summer session" was just an attempt to make up for time lost during the fall. Children rarely attended classes for more than six months in a year, compared to the full nine-month term back in Ohio.

Following his discharge from service after the war ended,

Will had found a job as lumber inspector for the Chapman and Dewey Lumber Company in Marked Tree. While he was at work inspecting timber, I went on an exploring expedition, handicapped to a certain extent by the vagaries of local transportation. One day I set out for Lepanto, a neighboring town about twelve miles away, on what was supposed to be the 2:30 P.M. train. A combination freight and passenger local, it switched around in the yard until about 4:00, then chugged a couple of miles out of Marked Tree and rested on a siding for over an hour. During the wait, several of us passengers went up to the engine and visited with the engineer and fireman. I reached my destination a little after 6:30 P.M. Another time this twelve-mile trip took an hour and twenty-eight minutes, because the train stopped eight times enroute, once pulling out of some tiny station along the way, then backing up several hundred feet as a brakeman on the platform waved frantically about some trivial matter or another. It was, to be sure, a heck of a way to run a railroad, but nobody seemed to mind much.

Will had heard about good farming lands around Lake City and Monette thirty miles to the north, where the sandy soil was more easily worked than the heavy gumbo around Marked Tree. I found that although they grew a greater variety of crops there, including watermelon and vegetables, the soil was less productive. When I reported this to Will, we agreed to concentrate our efforts in the Marked Tree area.

While looking over the situation, we ran across a banker named Henry Dilatush, who took us out south of town to see a quarter section he had for sale. Since the weather was exceptionally dry at that time of year, we were able to travel much of the distance by car, to within a mile or so of our destination. We little realized then — nor were we told — that for most of the year the road we had traveled would be altogether impassable, even for an agile Tin Lizzie. Sturdy mules pulling an empty wagon often

16

had trouble getting over the trail to Marked Tree. Only boats were practicable throughout the winter and spring.

Mr. Dilatush owned a half-section of heavily timbered gumbo land, of which we were offered 160 acres on the west. The thick growth of timber made it difficult for us to judge how the soil would serve for crops. If we'd had any sense, we would have looked for sweet gum trees, which grow best in a rich, porous soil. Wild cane is also a good indicator. As it turned out, both were scarce there, but we were just then entering the School of Hard Knocks and hadn't yet studied that lesson.

We were also poor bargainers and no doubt appeared over-anxious. This may have affected the asking price. When Dilatush mentioned $8,500, we accepted without much haggling. We were to find that our purchase was hardly a bargain, judged by then-prevailing prices, although the land — due to many factors — is worth several times that much today. At any rate, we became the proud, if somewhat naive, owners of a quarter-section of uncleared, uncultivated, unimproved Arkansas gumbo. The deed papers, pinpointing our location exactly, show that our new empire consisted of the "Southwestern quarter of Section 5, Township 9, Range 6 East, Crittenden County, Arkansas." The north border of our square tract lay exactly one-half mile south of Poinsett County, in which Marked Tree is located.

Our next step was to buy a team and wagon — and here we made a more profitable transaction. Back in town, Lew Williams, a trader of sorts, offered us a wagon and a span of mules with harness, all for $500. When he threw in an extra set of harness and agreed to a money-back guarantee, we accepted the deal. It proved to be a bargain; the mules, Sam and Rhody, turned out to be the best workers we ever had, and soon became prominent members of the "family."

Will quit his job with the lumber company, an axe was added to our equipment, and we hit the trail in the best traditions of Lewis and Clarke, Daniel Boone, and "Wagon-train."

The trip to our new homestead took longer than we had expected, because of the roads — or more exactly, the lack of them. Night began to fall while we were still two miles from our destination. We sought lodging at cabins along the trail, but were turned away. This, I think, was an exception rather than the rule; one of the chief characteristics of the people of the region is their instinctive hospitality. But they surely may be forgiven for being suspicious of us, two strange Yankees headed into the wilderness provisioned with little more than our trusty mule team and an axe.

We eventually came to a logging trail, which proved to be a blessing in disguise. A number of trees had recently been felled across the path, and we had to make frequent stops to clear them away with the axe, but following this route we finally came just after nightfall to a timber camp. Here we again echoed William Cowper's plea for "a lodge in some vast wilderness," and this time were made welcome. We learned to our surprise that our host, whom we had never met, was John Haverstick, a joint owner with his father and uncle of the newly-opened section just west of our own property.

He saw to it that our team was taken care of, although Will and I, used to handling only horses and knowing how they would fight each other, feared for the lives of our mules when they were put into a corral with many others. We were to learn that mules get along peacefully with strangers, even sharing the common feeding trough with them.

Then Mr. Haverstick had the camp's Negro cook prepare a "feeding trough" for Will and me, and we were given a pallet in one of the tents, with some oil of citronella to help keep the mosquitoes away. Next morning after a hearty breakfast, we were on our way again, refreshed and encouraged by the hospitality we had received. John and

18

the other Haversticks, who had come to Arkansas from Indiana only a few years earlier, continued to be most obliging, helpful neighbors in the years that followed.

When we reached our new home, there was little evidence that man had ever set foot there before. A few rusty and blackened tin cans at one spot showed where a passing party had once camped out; otherwise there were only some "marked trees," daubed with red paint to serve as boundary markers, a log-wagon trail, an abandoned log dump, and a few tree stumps left from cursory logging efforts some years before. New trees had grown up on the cut-over land, rejoining it to the surrounding wilderness of more than 8,000 acres. Dense, sparsely settled woodlands hemmed us on the south and east; the section to the west, owned by the Haversticks, was just being opened up, with a few houses going up and some ground already under cultivation; and on a quarter section to the north, owned by a Dr. Baird in Marked Tree, two houses had already been built and a start made at farming.

Thus Marked Tree and its environs became the center of our universe, and two more pioneers were added to the long list in American history.

III A LODGE IN THE WILDERNESS:

Home, Home on the Slough

Our first concern was for getting a roof over our heads. We made arrangements to stay with a family named Odum, who lived in the house nearest us on the north. Then we cleared a spot for a house and, while back in town for supplies, were able to hire a carpenter, Clyde Brooks, to help Will with the construction while I hauled building materials. Fortunately, there was a sawmill about four miles away where we could obtain most of the lumber, but for some of it, such as doors and windows, and for the tile flues, I had to make trips to Marked Tree.

A round trip normally required the better part of two days — and sometimes longer if things didn't go well, as often was the case. On one occasion when road conditions were even worse than usual, I made the trip into town, spent the night at Gamble's Boarding House, then loaded up my supplies early the next morning and started home about 10 A.M. I had tried to allow plenty of travel time, but the going was even slower than I had anticipated. Finally I reached a point about two miles from our place and decided to take a logging road, which grew increasingly less visible as I went along, until shortly it disappeared altogether. I had followed it the wrong way! Leaving the mules and wagon, I walked ahead to find the best route to a familiar place, and after charting a course I started back . . . but where the heck had I left that wagon and team? What direction to take? One who has never had such an experience can scarcely appreciate the complete bewilderment that accompanies a loss of orientation. All signs seem to fail.

After several fruitless expeditions, I finally found the mules and wagon, exactly where I had left them. In another half hour or so, we came to an unfamiliar but somewhat better road in the woods and seemed to be on our way, when suddenly the smaller mule, named Sam, keeled over in the traces. The poor fellow was completely exhausted and no doubt suffering from thirst, for in my concern for getting home I had neglected to water the team along the way.

I unhitched the mules from the wagon, and after finally getting Sam to his feet, we slogged on home in the dark, leaving the wagon behind to be recovered the next morning. The trip had taken nine hours.

It was while hauling supplies for the house that I first had occasion to observe one of the more peculiar traits of the people in our raw and secluded part of the world. I refer to the curious, paradoxical blend of gentleness and combustive violence to which so many of them seemed disposed. I was quickly impressed by the Southern hospitality of our new friends and neighbors; although sometimes shy with strangers, they were, almost without exception, generous and charitable, calm, temperate, and normally peaceful. Most of them we knew as rather religious, law-abiding citizens who worked hard, took care of their families, and helped their neighbors in time of trouble or need. Yet

21

many among them possessed an equally natural inclination to violence; a cold, blind, and fathomless fury that surged from instant hidden wells of frustration and affront. Shortly after we had begun work on our house, I was in Marked Tree to pick up some pieces of timber. Their size and shape made it necessary to have a longer reach, or coupling, for the wagon, and I was trying to dress one to fit, with an axe as my only tool. As I struggled away, a stranger walked by and, seeing how handicapped I was, suggested that I come with him to his house and get his saw and plane. I hesitated, fearing that I might damage or misplace them, but he insisted, and I finally accepted his offer. As we went to get the tools, he told me he had just lost his job to a "nigger," and was "going to get that black s.o.b." In a short while I finished my job and returned the man's tools, thankful for the lift he had given me.

I thought little of the incident until the next day, when I was back in town for another load of lumber and noticed some excitement downtown. Investigating, I learned that my Good Samaritan of the day before had encountered his man on the street, and without a word, had shot the Negro three or four times. Then he walked into a drugstore nearby, bought a cigar, sat down on the steps outside, and calmly had a smoke. Luckily the man's aim was as bad as his temper; the Negro had not been hit in a vital spot and lived through it all. The white man was eventually tried, but I did not learn what sentence, if any, he was given. When I last heard of him, he was town marshal in the still tougher town of Trumann, about fifteen miles away.

There was to be an almost endless number of even more violent incidents stemming from such relatively trivial grounds, involving "solid" citizens who were otherwise tranquil and humane. I don't know if any scholarly studies have been made of the subject, but surely it is fertile ground for sociological and psychological investigation.

I make no pretense of being any kind of authority on the matter, but it seems to me that certain factors and causes can be observed. Foremost was the rough, undeveloped nature of our region, involving as it did a shifting population of many diverse elements but mostly of the poorer classes, coming and going through the area as if it were a revolving door. Then too there was the lack of adequate law enforcement, aggravated by poor transportation and communication facilities.

Thus the very things — the poverty and remoteness and strangeness — which made the people dependent upon each other and so created their free-hearted, hospitable nature — these same things were largely responsible for the frustrations and antagonisms that led them to violence. I think, too, that the general atmosphere of the time cannot be ignored. It was a violent decade in American history, with gang wars raging in Chicago, labor riots in Pittsburgh, skirmishes with Prohibition agents all over the land. Lurid headlines — even in Marked Tree — touted the details of Sacco-Vanzetti, Snyder-Gray, Hall-Mills, Dempsey-Tunney, and a hundred lesser bloodlettings across the nation. This was heady enough stuff for local toughs, and some of it inevitably rubbed off on nearly everyone.

Finally, there was the matter of race — but surely that is a subject too immense and complex to deal with adequately or accurately here. Today we are more aware of the injustices and terribly oppressing conditions that have been imposed, violently and otherwise, upon the Negro. Surely racial hatreds were responsible for some of the trouble we knew of, but I'm convinced that all the encounters between white and Negro caused hardly a fraction of the damage by each to members of his own race.

To my knowledge, there were no lynchings or organized acts of violence against Negros during my time in the area. A story on the front page of the *Marked Tree Tribune* (not always noted for its liberality) for September 10, 1926, noted that Ku Klux Klan organizers had been seen in the area and deplored the Klan as "a scheme for lining the pockets of hoodlums, troublemakers and scum." Said the

23

writer, "We are confident it will find few adherents here, for it is one organization the residents of Marked Tree can do without."

Violence was usually man-to-man, and in any particular case it would be difficult to judge to just what extent prejudice or bigotry was a cause. No doubt the man who loaned me his tools was miffed that it was a Negro who had taken his job, but he would have shot a white "scab" just as readily.

At any rate, such goings-on would never have occurred in our older, more conservative Ohio country, where the people, while perhaps less outgoing, were given to settling their disputes peaceably. From this and later incidents I learned that such extremes of kindness and violence were to be expected in a brash and developing community like Marked Tree.

Before being distracted by blood and gore, I was discussing the developments we were planning back at the farm. We had selected, as the most logical place to build, a site on the east bank of a slough called Big Broadmouth. This slough, extending both above and below our place about two miles each way, is a depression some fifteen feet lower than the surrounding land and varying in width from four hundred to eight hundred feet. It is thought to have been caused by the New Madrid earthquakes in 1811 and 1812, when thousands of acres in Arkansas, Missouri, and Tennessee were sunk; and as late as 1815 it formed the meander line of the St. Francis. In it is a lake of several acres, mostly on our farm but extending northward into Dr. Baird's. This lake never goes dry, but in exceptionally dry weather a number of willow snags protrude above the water, like the heads of hippopotami.

We decided to locate our house near the southern end of the slough, at the point where it turns from its north-south course and begins to wander west, then back north again to the St. Francis about a mile away. We knew that here the slough would be flowing during the winter wet season, providing a plentiful water supply for the house as

24

well as access for boats when the trails and roads, such as they were, would be impassable.

Since it was already September when we bought the place and began to build, we worked in great haste to beat the onset of bad weather. We encountered a few setbacks, however. After two or three weeks our carpenter, Clyde Brooks, took off for town, supposedly only for a day or two. In the meantime Will and I fell victims to our own cooking (we diagnosed it as ptomaine poisoning from canned tomatoes that had spoiled) and became quite sick. I was in slightly better shape than Will and managed to go for medicine. In town I saw Clyde and realized that he hadn't intended to return as promised. I had almost exhausted my powers of persuasion when he finally agreed to come back with me on the boat.

Clyde was some character. Country people often speak of notorious but harmless liars as being "windy"; Clyde was windy. Once with a straight face he related the story of a backwoodsman in the area who, years before, had lived with his old woman and children in a hollow log. His worldly condition improved so that he acquired a hound dog and a shotgun. These he traded for a quarter section of land on which he built a rail pen where the family lived thereafter. The part of the story I found least credible was that a shiftless backwoodsman would ever part with his hound and shotgun.

With Will and me on our feet again and able to keep Clyde busy and pacified, we were able, despite our setbacks that fall, to finish not only the original structure, but a second one just like it, about four hundred feet south of the first.

These houses were of a rather conventional design, common to the better type of tenant houses in that country. They were constructed without any sort of formal plan; Will, whose versatility in many areas paid off for us again and again, supervised the layout and solved most of the incidental problems of construction.

Each house had three rooms, of box construction and erected on a foundation of pecky cypress blocks. Overall dimensions were 26 x 16 feet. The main room, extending across the sixteen-foot front, was fourteen feet deep, while the kitchen, directly behind, was 16 x 12. The walls of these two rooms were eight feet high, with a third room, a kind of overgrown attic, built directly over the main room, with identical floor dimensions but only five feet high at the eaves. A porch extended across the front. The siding was rough cypress, costing $35.00 per thousand board feet and battened with half-inch cypress strips three inches wide. The roofs were shingled. No thought was given to painting, inside or out. We installed tile chimneys which — as we shall see — proved to be a rather disastrous mistake. The total cost of each of these houses was slightly over $500 (not counting our labor) which was probably a little more than for the average dwelling of that type.

While the first house was under construction, Clyde, Will, and I boarded and lodged with neighbors — first with the Odum family on Baird's place north of us, then with the Harmon Smiths who lived in another house on the same farm. At the Odums we were often roused on chilly fall mornings by Old Man Odum starting a wood fire in the battered cook stove. Then he would go back to bed and call to his daughter, Etta, about sixteen: "Etter! Etter! Time to get up!" Then, while we grabbed a last wink or two, "Etter" would get up and prepare breakfast for all of us. One day, rather wistfully, Etta mentioned that she had not been to town since August 20, 1918 — over thirteen months earlier. No wonder she knew the exact date!

I remember our stay with Harmon Smith and his wife primarily because of the mild shock Will and I experienced when Mrs. Smith proceeded to nurse their baby at the table while we ate. Our sheltered Yankee lives had hardly prepared us for such casual intimacy among strangers, but apparently it was a good Southern custom. Later, on several occasions in Marked Tree, I saw mothers nursing their babies while walking along the crowded main street.

With our first house finished, we scraped together enough odds and ends of furniture to "make do" and moved in, while work continued on the second house. Clyde stayed with us until it was almost finished.

Next our attention turned to a water supply. We had at first carried our drinking water from the Baird place when we came to work on the houses. Then we put down a driven well, which is exactly what its name implies — a piece of pipe driven into the ground until it strikes a good vein of water (usually twelve to fifteen feet, but we encountered the usual Swank luck and had to go down to twenty). As the well is being driven, the threads at the upper end of the pipe are protected by a wooden block which is later removed so that a pitcher pump may be screwed onto the pipe.

Well-water on the adjoining Baird farm was pure and clear, and ours appeared that way at first, but after pumping out a few buckets, we discovered that a standing bucketful would develop an oily scum on it after a few minutes, then in the center it would turn opaque to the bottom, and soon the darkening would spread throughout the bucket. A well at the second house turned out just as bad. Later we tried running the well water through a so-called water-softener jar — a device consisting of two upright porcelain containers, one inside the other, the smaller of which, holding three or four gallons, was of a porous nature, allowing the water to filter through slowly and rejuvenating it in the process. This worked well enough for a short time, but the inside jar soon became too coated to be of use, and we discarded it. Fortunately, rains soon came, and the slough had plenty of good water in it for several months. Eventually our taste buds seemed to accommodate themselves to the well water, and thus we had a year-round supply — slough water in winter and well water in summer. Our stomachs somehow remained usable, and even seemed to acquire a certain tolerance for brackishness.

We had hardly gotten settled in our new home when we acquired several hundred "guests" — a big herd of goats which insisted on taking shelter under our house at night. You can't appreciate the situation unless you've ever tried to sleep with a flock of goats in your basement. Of course, we had no basement as such. The house was built up several feet off the ground on cypress blocks, allowing room for the goats to shinny in underneath. The goat smell was bad enough, but what really disturbed us was the almost continual butting of their horns against the floor. I could never understand why they were so restless, unless mosquitoes were to blame.

The goats belonged to the Haversticks, who had conceived the idea of using the animals to clear land economically. Goats of course eat almost anything, and they're particularly fond of leaves and twigs. I have even seen them on inclined tree trunks, climbing up to munch vines and leaves several feet from the ground. The Haversticks also figured the goats would keep down new undergrowth as well as clearing off the virgin stand, but they failed to reckon with a number of factors. First was the wetness of the ground; many of the animals took colds and died. Predators, such as dogs and wolves, also exacted a heavy toll, and soon the rank odors and wild thumpings no longer emanated from beneath our floor. A promising venture had proved decidedly unprofitable. (A similar experiment has been more successful. Today farmers in the area use geese to hoe their cotton. The geese gobble up every weed in sight but, strange as it seems, leave the cotton plants untouched.)

We were less imaginative than the Haversticks, and relied on more conventional labor to clear our land. While we were putting up the first house and staying with the

28

Odums, we had hired Old Man Odum's son Herbert, about eighteen, to do some clearing for us. It was hardly more profitable than the goat venture, for Herbert apparently had some principles against stooping: he cut the brush so high and left so much standing that we had to cut it all over again. He hadn't piled what he cut, either, and we had to do that too, in order to burn it. But things have a way of happening in cycles, in and out, down and up, bad and good. Our next employee was a great deal more competent.

IV WOUNDS OF MEN AND OF TREES:

We Find a New Friend, Clear the Land, and Endure a Disaster

The winter of 1919-1920 was spent clearing new ground, a task which involves perhaps the most onerous and splendid labor known to man. In this we were fortunate to have with us as friend, employee, co-worker, companion, and philosopher, a tough old gentleman named George Keth.

Mr. Keth (to us he was never "George" but always "Mr. Keth") belonged to that special breed of men outside the common herd — lost and lonely men who inhabit small towns and nameless backwaters, moving by sidewinds across the land, from yard to dock to field. I do not mean to imply that he was a tramp or hobo, for although he had come far from his Pennsylvania Dutch origins and left native roots to wither, his manner evoked a permanence, a sense of place, that floaters never have. He had once been married — "it didn't take," he said, and he had a crusty bachelor's aversion to women, of whom he gruffly and frequently remarked, "They are helpeats, not helpmeets" — and he had lived a number of years in Henderson, Kentucky, before somehow following the trail to Marked Tree. Kentucky remained his blood's country; he still dwelt there in his dreams.

A number of things distinguished Mr. Keth from the ordinary frontier drifter. He was a small, neat man with a proud moustache, and he carried himself with an erect dignity that commanded respect, even when he was several sheets in the wind — for like many of his kind, Mr. Keth relieved his aching drab world with transient splendors from a jug. But he studiously confined his drinking to periodic sprees. He always combed his hair carefully before meals — an amenity few of the natives practiced — and made an unobtrusive but almost philosophical ritual of smoking his pipe after eating.

History and literature abound with the likes of George Keth. Real life acknowledges only those few who, touched by some Fate or another, rise to greater heights; but fiction — more often true than strange, to twist the saw — has given us the common, throbbing Mr. Keths. I think of Mr. Micawber and Tristram Shandy's Uncle Toby, even Falstaff, perhaps, without the padding . . . in a nearer time and place, Wolfe's Oliver Gant and V. K. Ratliff of Yoknapatawpha County. Perhaps it would be more nearly accurate to say that I envision Mr. Keth as the kind of man Huckleberry Finn grew up to be. It was partly out of respect for his age (we considered him old, but he was only in his early fifties) partly because of his bearing that we always addressed him as *Mr.* Keth; but that, I think, says a great deal about the kind of man he was.

We first became acquainted with Mr. Keth during the time we were building our houses. He was employed then by Dr. Baird and was clearing new ground on the doctor's place adjoining ours. He started the same kind of work for Will and me in mid-December of 1919, and stayed with us off and on until 1924, proving to be a most competent and versatile hand, if perhaps a bit erratic.

Mr. Keth was a whiz at ground-clearing. He hated cross-cut saws, but was a real axe man — the only person I ever knew who could swing one equally well right- or left-handed. He would cut right-handed halfway through a standing tree, then reverse hands, chop from the other side, and make the two cuts meet exactly. This makes the direction of fall more difficult to gauge, but he gloried in a neat stump.

One time he found a small elm tree with a swollen section halfway up the trunk. He cut out a three-and-a-half-foot length of it with the enlarged bole in the center and carried it to the house, heavy as it was. Then he and my brother made a table top for it and we were all as proud of it as if it were a Chippendale or Sheraton period piece.

When we needed a bridge across Little Broadmouth — an offshoot of the bigger slough, running across our farm — Mr. Keth and I placed logs across the banks as support, and he made the bridge floor, splitting small logs into puncheons eight or nine feet long and laying them, smooth center side up, across the supporting logs to make a uniform surface.

Big Broadmouth slough, running in front of our house, was four hundred to eight hundred feet wide, much of it grown up in shrubs and tangles. In front of our house we cut a strip across the slough so that during high water we could get across in the little boat we kept tied up on our bank. Frequently someone from the opposite side would call across for one of us to bring the boat over so he could cross to our side.

One day when the slough was full of water, Mr. Keth heard a voice on the other side calling to him. He recognized it as that of someone he disliked. For all his gruffness, the old fellow had a wry sense of humor.

The voice called, "Bring the boat over here."

"The boat is over here," Mr. Keth called back.

"Yes, but I want to get across the slough."

"Well, you *are* across the slough."

"Yes, but I want over there."

"Well, you *are* over there," Mr. Keth again informed him.

"Yes, but bring the boat over to this side so I can get over to that side."

"Friend," came Mr. Keth's final answer, "the boat *is* over on this side and you *are* over on that side." And he never made a move toward the boat.

The wonder is that the fellow didn't jump in, swim across, and tackle the old man. We concluded from this episode that one's point of view — in a larger sense as well — is influenced by who you are and where you are.

After a few weeks at swinging an axe, Mr. Keth would grow restive, and we knew he was about to take off on a drinking spree. He would make some excuse to go to town, and then return after a few days, looking considerably worse for wear but raring to swing the axe again. Occasionally, when there was a brief letup in the work, he would obtain liquor from some moonshiner near the farm and then lie around practically dead to the world, refusing all food and aid. Sometimes he lay stretched out under the house but more often reeled stiffly away some distance into the woods before collapsing. At times we feared he might pass out permanently. Mr. Keth took his work seriously, whether chopping or drinking.

The clearing days were hard and dull. We got out of bed by 5:30, had breakfast — which of course we had to fix ourselves — washed the dishes, and were swinging axes by 7:00. One of us would quit an hour or so before noon to fix dinner; then after eating and dishwashing we were at it again, often until dark. I can recall washing supper dishes by lamplight. This routine varied little from winter to summer.

Brush clearing is not a game for novices. For example, it took us a while — and some pain — to learn that although everything else had to be cut low, cane must be left standing at least half a foot high so that mules' hooves would strike the stalk and deflect, rather than coming down on top of the sharp, tough cane ends. I still have a knee scar attesting to the same danger to humans who stumble and fall on the cane stubs. Everything we cut (except of course the salable trees) was put into piles and burned — but only with much difficulty because of the dampness. Fortunately that first winter was unusually mild, and we worked in our shirt sleeves most of the time.

We found the Arkansas flora strangely different from what we had known back home. In Ohio the Virginia creeper grows meekly in its proper place, but here it spread riotously wherever it could get a foothold. We saw it by the thousand as weeds in cornfields. The matted vines created great problems with the clearing work, as did the possum grapes. The latter resemble our northern wild grapes in taste and appearance, but proved to be a much greater nuisance in Arkansas. The bittersweet vine, found almost everywhere, is, I think, the meanest of all in the work of clearing new ground.

Things went well through the winter, but on the first day of March, 1920, disaster struck — not quite fatal, as it turned out, but unnerving enough at the time. On that day, with our clearing work well underway, we had arranged for Jesse White, a Negro who worked for Dr. Baird, to come with his three heavy mules and pull off ("snake" was the term we loggers used) unsalable logs to be piled and burned. We hoped to accomplish a great deal that day, and perhaps our misfortune was the result of undue eagerness and misplaced haste. At any rate, Will and Mr. Keth had felled a tree and were trimming it up, when Mr. Keth, working near the smaller end, cut away a short branch which, unknown to him, had been supporting the trunk. This caused the tree to turn at the exact instant that Will struck with his own axe. The blade missed the tree, and Will's left foot took the full force of the axe swing, cutting on top of it the full width of the axe and to the sole underneath. Will instantly tore off his shirt for a tourniquet, which we tied tightly below his knee. Jesse hoisted Will to his back and carried him to the mule shed, almost a quarter-mile away, where I bridled Sam and Rhody. Will and I, followed by our faithful collie, Sport, rode off to Luttrell's Landing — about two miles away through the woods — in hope of getting a boat to Marked Tree. We paused only briefly to loosen, then tighten the tourniquet, but by the time we reached the landing, Will was quite weak from loss of blood.

We soon located a man named Parrott, a rather tough river character who sported two or three recent bullet wounds in his face and neck. He owned a small speedboat, and we persuaded him to rush Will to town.

On my way back to the farm with the two mules and our collie — a gift at Christmas from our folks back in Ohio — I noticed that the dog was frothing at the mouth, a sure sign of black-tongue disease, for which there is no cure. Sport had shown great aptitude as a stock dog and was far and away the best pup we'd ever had.

But the Fates still weren't through with us. The third blow came that afternoon, when Mr. Keth and I were sawing down a hackberry tree. Instead of leaving a half-inch or so on his side to keep the tree from twisting as it fell, Mr. Keth — perhaps subconsciously moved by his hatred of saws — cut up to the notch, so that the falling tree twisted and pinched the saw, ruining it completely. We had paid eight dollars for it and were using it for the first time. I began to wonder if we had antagonized some timber god or been hexed by a backwoods witch doctor.

At a hospital in Memphis, my brother was given ether and sewn up, seven stitches being required to close the broad wound. Will amazed the operating doctor by reciting, while under ether, the entire Oath of Hippocrates, apparently the result of his unusual memory and a fondness he had once had for reading encyclopedias and old medical books. In ten or twelve days he was back home and able to walk a little with the aid of crutches.

In the meantime, however, Mr. Keth had gone off on one of his sprees, and I was left alone. While out snaking off some logs one day, I was caught in a sudden rainstorm. Hurrying the team toward shelter with one hand and carrying the double-bitted axe over my shoulder with the other, I fell over a vine, driving an axe blade into the back of my neck. I tied up the mules and hurried through the woods to Harmon Smith's house, holding a handkerchief to my neck to staunch the flow of blood. Despite the handkerchief, I managed to leak enough blood for a massacre or two, with maybe an old-fashioned saloon brawl thrown in, and Mrs. Smith was sure I'd been mortally wounded. But she applied a bandage of sorts and I soon recovered, with only a small permanent scar as a memento.

With Will hobbling around on crutches and me holding my head like a piece of rare china, the firm of Swank Brothers Land, Cattle, and General All-Round Batching Company was pretty much out of business for awhile. There is some evidence, however, that things were not too bad. While we were recuperating, Will wrote to our folks in Ohio, beginning in his typically whimsical fashion: "Now that I'm taking a rest, I'll try to make up for past neglect in writing, and maybe get a little ahead, so that I can lie down on the job later on."

V PLOWING NEW GROUND:

Old Roots Are Torn Up, New Ones Put Down

In *The Bothie of Tober-na-Vuolich,* one of the better narrative poems of the nineteenth century, Arthur Clough wrote, "Let us to Providence trust and abide and work in our stations." I suppose that's pretty good advice for almost any occasion, and we generally tried to follow it in one way or another. I don't mean that we tacked it up on the wall or went around quoting it to each other — I'm not even sure we were much aware of Mr. Clough at the time — but we did try to keep our heads up and do our work; and during the time Will and I were convalescing from our axe wounds, we leaned pretty hard on that part about trust and abide, for we did not have too large a selection of other things from which to choose. We managed to work in our stations, too, for there we had a larger choice. So many things needed to be done, practically all of which

37

were work, that if we did anything at all we were performing labor in some "station" or another.

One of my stations was that of cook. We had planned to alternate in the kitchen each week, but it didn't work out that way. For a number of seemingly complex reasons which I never quite figured out, I found myself doing kitchen police with increasing frequency. The fact that Will was bigger than I was may have had something to do with it.

Cooking was not a lost art with us, for we had never acquired it. We had everything to learn, and I suspect it was much more difficult back then to acquire the rudiments of food preparation than it would be now, considering the accumulation of newly developed, pre-mixed, and even pre-cooked foods. Who in 1920 would have dreamed of instant mashed potatoes; instant tea and coffee; powdered milk; hash, stew, pancake, cornbread, and cake mixes; canned chicken and ham — to make only a partial list of the many convenient, flavorful foods available today. Some innovations, like TV dinners, would not have helped us much, for of course we had no refrigeration; but all of the other things I've mentioned would have kept quite awhile without it.

At first we took care to buy our supplies in "sufficient quantities" — as if preparing for a famine or suddenly sky-rocketing prices. On one occasion I bought a hundred pounds of navy beans and a little later the same amount of rice. I used about the same restraint in preparing the first meal of rice, little realizing how it would swell up. I had to scurry around to find containers to hold it all. We ate mostly rice for several weeks. Fortunately, we were able to unload some of the beans and rice — at reduced rates — to the Haversticks, who ran a commissary for their share-croppers and thus had a ready market for foods in such bulk.

A friend with whom I had taught school back in Ohio proved the old saw about a friend in need being a friend indeed when she sent us a cookbook. It was a paperback entitled *The Handbook of Recipes,* by Faith Robinson

38

Lanham, full of advice and "down-to-earth" recipes that almost literally proved to be lifesavers. We might not have starved without them, but we were skirting the seas of malnutrition when the book arrived.

Food value and even taste were, however, almost secondary considerations to us. We were interested in convenience and speed. We learned that Irish potatoes boiled faster in the jackets if a ring were peeled around them. We found a mince meat preparation that was sold in boxes and could be transformed into pies with little trouble. And we discovered the virtues of a one-can, one-course meal — salmon or vegetable soup or tomatoes popped right out of a can and eaten without much ceremony or preparation. It was no culinary feat, other than that it filled an empty space, but on hot, busy days it saved a lot of anguish over stove and dishpan.

All of our Arkansas neighbors depended on home-made biscuits for their bread supply. We soon learned to make them, mixing up the dough by hand — a rather messy, time-consuming job — then pinching off and shaping each piece for the pan. Almost seven years later I learned from an old bachelor who worked for Dr. Baird that there was an easier way to make biscuits. He used a softer batter, mixing it up with a ladle, then spooned it out as biscuits or bread into the baking pan. This required but a little time, and I thought the spooned bread really tasted better.

We usually tried to grow a garden to supply fresh vegetables. A garden crop we particularly liked was one entirely new to us. This was okra, which thrived in the area. After we'd grown it a year or two, it began to choose its own garden spots, stalks of it springing up voluntarily ("volunteer" was the country adverb and adjective) close by the kitchen door. In soup, or sliced and fried crisp in flour, it was delicious.

We had labored desperately all through the early months of 1920, hoping to have enough land cleared to start a crop in the spring. By April we had several acres ready, but Will was still laid up with his wound, and I was busy holding things together, trying to keep us fed, see after the stock, and continue with the clearing operations whenever I could. Thus we arranged for a fellow named Clarence Hahn to make a share crop for us on the land we'd cleared.

This was ground the plow of man had never touched. The procedure in working it was first to use a stock — a straight shovel plow — to lay off the cotton rows, then list with a Vulcan "new ground" plow, throwing two rows together, then bedding this up with one more furrow on each side turned toward the first two. The ground was so wet and so full of roots that one could scarcely tell where the rows were supposed to be. And the work was painfully slow, for the team was stopped by roots every ten or fifteen feet. Clarence was a husky, hulking brute, but he grew discouraged. Finally he came to us and said, "I give up. How much do I owe you?" We felt that we owed him instead, and so we paid him about twenty dollars for his labor and regretfully watched him depart. With some misgivings (for I weighed at least fifty pounds less than Clarence) I tackled the barely half-completed task and managed to finish it.

That spring we put in an acre of cotton and two or three acres of corn. Will, still on crutches, managed to help me with the corn planting, hobbling along and dropping the grains after I had marked out the rows. Strangely enough, in view of the dense vegetation that had previously been rooted where we made the plantings, the crop was remarkably free of weeds and easy to work. This is a peculiar phenomenon of the first year's cultivation, for aside from the vines I've mentioned, weeds don't grow much in wooded areas. Wind, birds, and time are needed to give them a real start. I've seen good first-year corn crops made without any cultivation or hoeing whatever. It's a different story later on, when cockleburs and other "volunteer" foliage become quite troublesome. Just as it seemed to take weeds a year to find us in the woods, the same was true with

40

flies and sparrows. Although we had new problems to cope with, we at least had a respite from some old, established ones.

In May we had our first visit from a member of the family. Mother's brother, Uncle Howard Doughty, who lived in Casper, Wyoming, was looking for a place to retire away from the rigors of Wyoming winters, and he traveled out to look over northeast Arkansas. One hot, humid day he arrived at the farm frayed to a frazzle, having trudged all the way out from Marked Tree wearing his heavy Wyoming-winter underwear. Dismayed at the constant spring rains and the utter fatigue of our frontier life, he was soon ready to head back to Wyoming, blizzards or no blizzards.

Uncle Howard may also have been disturbed by our isolation and remoteness from "civilization," even though he was there during the season when transportation facilities were at their best. From May to November we could usually get to Marked Tree by land. Our route was through the woods to Luttrell's Landing, then along the river over a rutted trail — it would be the grossest kind of exaggeration to call it a road — to a point two or three miles outside town where we angled back northeast to the Black Oak Road and thence north into town. The exact route over the trail varied, for we tried from time to time to pick the best course available under existing conditions. The only stretch constantly in use was a half mile or so where sawmill slabs had been laid down close together through a marshy area. Near our end of the trail was a Negro church, a sort of shed, with a circular saw blade mounted on its edge to serve as a bell.

Later, two and a half miles of east-west roadway were cleared, straight through from Luttrell's Landing to the Black Oak School (for white children). From this point the Black Oak Road stretched north about five miles into Marked Tree. Two miles above Black Oak (a place name with no "place" other than the school at that time) on the way to town stood a Negro school.

Sometime in the early twenties, a man named Smith contracted to make a road levee just outside town along our route and went broke in the attempt. I recall seeing many Negros and mules at work with small dump shovels, dragging little, seemingly endless loads of dirt up the slopes and dumping them on the road bed.

The road that resulted was still impassable after rains, which simply turned it into a mound of mucky gumbo. In preference to slogging through with a wagon we sometimes walked all the way to town in hip boots, tiresome as it was. The trick was to avoid lifting one's foot suddenly and to walk in puddles whenever possible, where the water helped loosen the gumbo. Agricultural experts have referred to it as a "black, waxy soil," and its stickiness is proverbial. I got enough of it to last a lifetime one winter when I helped Uncle George Haverstick move ten wagonloads of household goods some four miles over raw, wet roads having a consistency approximately that of a soggy sweetroll (the metaphor is inexact; there was nothing sweet about it). Four mules pulling a wagon only one-third full would bog down, and the driver had to poke, pry, push, and cuss the mud off the wheels.

As boys back in our Ohio hills, Will and I were always throwing stones — at targets, cows, birds, and each other (I remember once catching behind the ear, while in full retreat, a huge specimen of Ohio geology that almost laid me out for good). Rocks were as much a part of our lives in Ohio as the air we breathed, and, in an evil way, almost as necessary. Thus it was with a sense of amazement that, after twenty-two months in the delta lowlands of Arkansas, I wrote home:

> Since coming to Arkansas I have seen thousands of acres of land, but until last month there was something I had never seen — a stone! In fact, I finally saw a good many of them, at a tiny mound — or sandblow — on the Cummins farm not far away, and since then

have found one stone on a farm adjoining our own. A sharecropper's boy even found a stone on our own place. None would weigh more than a few ounces.

Sometime later I was helping a little neighbor boy, about seven years old, with a slingshot he was making. I told him that boys back home used stones as ammunition, and he asked, frowning, "What is *stones?*" I suppose the poor child had never seen one. When we finished the slingshot, he made a mud ball for it out of gumbo, which, either soft or in hard clods, is the nearest thing to a rock in the delta. Other substitutes used by youngsters were sticks and pieces of tree roots, of which there were plenty in our time, when so much of the land was just being cleared. The most common everyday Ohio pebble would be a "precious stone" to any boy in the lowlands. A geologist in search of rocks to study would most assuredly have been out of luck around our place.

VI COTTON AND 'CROPPERS:

A Saga of People Against
"A Bug Long Years Ago"

In the fall of 1920 we harvested our first cotton crop, which yielded the whopping sum total of one bale. It brought slightly over one hundred dollars, which we felt was very little for all of our labor. We had picked it with infinite care to avoid sullying the white lint with a single leaf or stem, and that in itself proved to be a foolish waste of time, for it did not materially affect the price at all.

Today most of the cotton in the area is harvested by machines, but of course we did it all by hand, stooping or crawling along the seemingly endless rows, dragging from the shoulder a nine-foot canvas sack whose weight always increased in reverse proportion to the worker's ability to pull it. A good picker could sometimes sack a hundred and twenty-five pounds a day, but that meant keeping the back bent and the hands and fingers flying, and it was done at

44

the expense of raw, swollen fingers and an all-over throbbing numbness that sapped every muscle and nerve-end and brain cell in your body. Later, as ginning methods and seed strains improved, harvest hands pulled off and sacked the whole cotton pod, boll and all, instead of laboriously plucking the lint out of the dried, sharply-pointed burr, as we had done. "Pulling bolls" was faster and easier on the hands; some workers could pull five or six hundred pounds a day. Huddie Ledbetter ("Leadbelly") writes of picking a thousand pounds a day in Texas, but I think he must have been "pulling" rather than "picking." At any rate, as Leadbelly says, "You can't fool around and pick a thousand pounds of cotton a day . . . you've got to jump around to get it." (Hence his song, "Jump down turn around, pick a bale of cotton . . . pick a bale a day.")

Whether picking or pulling, the job of harvesting cotton required a terrible lot of bending and crawling and clutching. I don't suppose it was any more tiring than cutting timber, but at least you could stand firm on your feet to cut a tree and take some pride in swinging the axe well. There was something faintly ignoble about picking cotton, being as it was a form of labor that put a man on his knees before a dinky, whithered stalk bearing fruit he couldn't eat, drink, or build a house out of. Yet the job had its redeeming features, too. Other farm work was pretty solitary — most of it involving only you and a mule or two — but harvesting cotton was an exception. It was the one job where you usually had some human companionship, and the burden of the cotton sack was eased to a great extent by the camaraderie which prevailed among the workers. Also, the harvest crew usually engaged in a sort of friendly rivalry to see who could pick the most, and there was the pleasant ritual of "weighing up" and keeping careful accounts to determine the winners. Then, too, fall was the best time of year with regard to weather conditions, and we normally enjoyed a respite from heavy rains, heat, and humidity during most of the harvest season.

45

By planting time in the spring of 1921, we had cleared about thirty acres — much more than we could farm ourselves. So we acquired a sharecropper named Frank Walters, who during the previous year had made a share crop on Dr. Baird's place north of us.

In that country — and I believe generally throughout the South — there were two predominant forms of tenant farming. If the renter furnished his own equipment and supplies, he paid the owner only one-third of his corn crop and one-fourth of his cotton crop. This was called "renting on the third and fourth." But if the owner furnished the mules and tools, he received as his share one-half the cotton and corn; this was sharecropping or "renting on the halves." With one or two exceptions, we usually followed this latter arrangement, and it was the one we made with Frank Walters. He seemed glad to get it, perhaps because the deal included a tenant house. At that time, Frank, his wife, and their two children were living with another family of five — the Jim Booths — in a tiny two-room houseboat that had been floated down Big Broadmouth slough during high water and grounded on Dr. Baird's farm a few hundred feet from our property line, near the junction of Little and Big Broadmouth.

The houseboat was approximately fourteen feet wide and twenty-six feet long, containing a bedroom-living room and kitchen, with tiny porches fore and aft. Toilet facilities were provided by the banks of Little Broadmouth with some flanking bushes and a few trees nearby. The structure was distinguished only by a thin coat of paint, which made it quite unique in that part of the woods. Needless to say, living conditions had been rather crowded with nine people sleeping in one small room.

Frank was the kind of fellow known locally as "a good old boy." A thin, sallow "country" man, he was good-natured and likeable, in a whimsical sort of way. I credited him with a quick intelligence, although it didn't always show

46

in the way he ran his family and his affairs. I recall the first time he came to our house, with a limp "roll-your-own" cigarette dangling from his lip. Behind him was his little boy, four or five years old, taking big steps to keep up and puffing on a corncob pipe for all he was worth. Later Will mentioned it to Frank, who agreed the boy "aurght not to have the habit," and they talked to the boy so threateningly as to scare him out of using tobacco — for a few years at least.

I remember Mrs. Walters mostly as a kind, homely woman with badly decayed teeth, a condition all too common in a region where a dentist would have been as rare a sight as a dodo to the deep woods people. While they were living on our farm, Mrs. Walters lost a baby in childbirth. There was no mention of a funeral or burial, and we did not ask. The several thousand acres of woodland around us offered ample burial ground; and it was out of the question to get an undertaker to come there. They managed the situation privately, with no outside attention expected or given.

That year Frank planted nearly five acres in corn and six or seven acres in cotton. All his sowing, however, was not confined to the soil.

There was a girl of sixteen or seventeen in a family who lived in the woods on Dr. Baird's farm, adjoining the land Frank was farming for us. As Frank and the mule plowed by the woods on summer days, she would come to the edge of the clearing and whistle. "Well, natcherly," said Frank later, "that mule was tard and needed a rest." Soon the girl was in a family way, and Frank was on the dodge.

He had a rather uncanny way of showing up at our house at mealtimes, even in the fall after Will and I had moved temporarily into a newly-built house on the far corner of our farm. Although it was now much farther to come, Frank showed up one evening when we were about to sit down to eat. Just then Will saw the whistling neighbor girl's father coming across the field with a shotgun. A passing

47

hunter had left a .30-30 deer rifle with us temporarily. Frank grabbed it and ran upstairs.

We nervously greeted the girl's father and invited him to supper. To our dismay, he accepted, and we sat down to what was for Will and me a most suspenseful meal. As we were finishing, we noticed some stray cattle nearby, and Will, knowing that our caller had recently lost several head, suggested that we go out and look them over. Then, making some excuse, he went upstairs and whispered to Frank to make his getaway while we were out. Frank needed little urging; we later learned that he passed his own house in a gust of dust and stopped only when he'd reached the Haversticks a half mile beyond, where he spent the night without any supper.

The father never mentioned to us his daughter or her condition. Apparently he carried the shotgun merely in case he ran across any game on his stroll. It seems there was no further involvement, domestic or pecuniary, as far as Frank was concerned.

The cotton boll weevil inflicted serious damage on the crop that season of 1921. Cotton was also infested with army worms, for the first time in that section, I believe. They can strip the cotton of all its foliage in a few days, but if this happens late enough in the season — and they were rather late that year — they may prove beneficial, in causing the cotton to open up well ahead of the frost. It interested me to see the hordes of worms leave a ravaged field, all crawling along in the same direction — truly an army of foragers.

Indirectly also, the boll weevil helped a bit by cutting the country's cotton production to about half the expected crop, thus raising the general run of prices for a time. Frank's six or seven acres of cotton produced three and a half bales. The first bale, weighing 510 pounds, sold for 21⅛ cents a pound; the second weighed 540 pounds and brought 17¾ cents a pound. Then prices slumped to below 15 cents.

48

During that year Will and I stayed busy with the clearing work. We also put in one acre of millet and over six acres of corn, which yielded enough to tide us over until the next season's crop.

In the early fall of 1921, we started work on a barn and a third house. The barn was about 30 x 40 feet — a post barn with framing of oak — located between our two houses on Big Broadmouth. The third house, identical to the other two, was built about half a mile away, on the southwest corner of our place. When we drove a well pipe there we were fortunate in finding much better drinking water.

It was pretty much all work and no play for awhile. Writing home shortly after Christmas of 1921, I made light of our hardships and spoke facetiously of the way young ladies were attracted to me. On Christmas Day I had been presented with an elegant bouquet of artificial roses by one of them — the Haverstick's Negro cook. Otherwise the holiday went mostly unnoticed. Will was in town and the only neighbors I saw that day were the cook and a Negro man with her.

Another young lady took quite a fancy to me and cried when I left her house one day. In fact, she tried to follow me home. She was little Miss Barham, about four years old, whose family had just moved onto our farm.

For over two months during that winter of 1921-22, my brother, like Job, was sorely afflicted with boils — about twenty in all. A few were on his wrists and hands, but most of them were on the back of his neck, causing even his face to swell so much he was unable to work part of the time.

Early in 1922 we arranged to let out the farm to two families of white renters from Hattiesburg, Mississippi. Just as Moses and Joshua had sent men on ahead to "spy out the land," these folks sent part of their number to our country with the idea of looking over the rich delta land, as we ourselves had done. Friends told us about them, and we soon made a deal with them to rent our farm "on the third and fourth."

They made the trip by covered wagon — three covered wagons, in fact, each pulled by two horses. It took them twelve days to travel the three hundred miles from Hattiesburg to Marked Tree. The trail they followed from Marked Tree to the farm covered twelve miles and accounted for a whole day of travel, for the roads — where they existed — were almost impassable on account of winter rains. Except for lurking Indians, this latter-day wagon train faced every hardship known to pioneers of old.

One of the two families was that of Mr. and Mrs. Russ Barham, who, with their four children and Mrs. Barham's brother, Lee Grafton, thirty-five, moved into our south house on the slough. In our first house, just north, were Vernon Grafton, twenty-eight, his wife Luna, and his two brothers, Tommy, twenty-one, and Dick, nineteen. The three Grafton boys were half-brothers of Lee and Mrs. Barham.

Shortly after they arrived, Russ Barham had a severe attack of appendicitis. He was rushed by boat to Marked Tree and from there by car to the hospital in Memphis. An incision revealed that his appendix had already burst, but he recovered in fine shape.

Meanwhile, the others pitched in to help with land clearing. Two years earlier we had paid $2.50 per day and board for clearing work, but the new renters did it for half that, and boarded themselves. Part of the clearing work was done at the flat rate of $20.00 an acre. All trees above twenty inches in diameter were allowed to stand.

Within two months the Barhams and Graftons had cleared over five acres, taken off many remaining trees on land previously cultivated, and plowed fifteen or twenty acres of new ground. Later, during the summer "lay-by" season — when the crop has been cultivated the last time and there's nothing to do until it "makes" and can be harvested — they cleared a stretch of woods a half mile long

50

and sixty feet wide for a projected new road directly east of our south line. They were tremendous workers.

By this time their money had run out and we had to "furnish" them. This was a common practice, consisting in the owner's making advancements to sharecroppers or renters, to be deducted from the gross crop income in the fall; it is, in other words, a levy against the crop. These advancements may be in money or — most often — on a store charge account backed by the owner. If the owner has a commisary, the tenant obtains whatever he needs on "time," or on a lien against the crop. Some owners with commissaries reportedly laid in profit coming and going by putting excessive prices on the goods they sold tenants — Faulkner's Ab Snopes accused Varner of "furnishing in six-bit dollars" — but I never personally knew of such an operation.

That spring the Barhams and Graftons had planted forty or forty-five acres in cotton and ten to fifteen acres in corn. But by that season, the boll weevil — a serious threat in previous years — had become really destructive. As I recall, their cotton yield in the fall was a scant ten bales, one-fourth of which went to us in rent. Such a low return was quite discouraging to hard workers like the Barhams and Graftons, even though the light crop throughout the South again meant higher prices. They almost literally got only peanuts for their labor — Vernon Grafton raised eight bushels of "goobers" on a tiny plot of ground not much bigger than a flower pot. It was about the only luck they had that year.

During this summer of 1922 we began work on our fourth, and last, house. It was erected not far from the third one, on the south line of the farm so as to face the projected road extension. The floor plan and general construction of this house were identical to the other three, except that for a part of the roof we used cypress shingles, called shakes, which we rived, or split, with a mallet and frow. In doing this one keeps taking off shingle-thick slices from the block, not from center to circumference, but from one side, then another, the block growing smaller and

51

smaller and the shingles more narrow. I did much of this while Will and a renter or two assisted the carpenter.

Also, we decided to use brick instead of tile for the chimney of this house. Thus several hundred brick (if I recall correctly, it was four hundred) had to be hauled by wagon from Marked Tree. Since it was summertime and at the height of the dry season, most of the trail was in fairly good condition. However, no grading had been done on the two-and-a-half-mile stretch between Black Oak Road and Luttrell's Landing, and the route was dotted with gaping holes where stumps had been removed. When I tried to cross a watery swale about two hundred feet wide, the brick-filled wagon bogged down under the heavy load. So I unloaded the bricks, an armload at a time, wading through the water — some of it knee-deep — to the other side, returning time and again until I had carried most of the load across. Finally the mules were able to start the now almost-empty wagon moving again. Of course, there was the reloading on the other side — and we soon came to another swale where the whole process had to be repeated. These are the things that try men's souls — or at least their endurance.

The lack of roads had always been a problem, and as the scope of our farming operations grew, it became a serious handicap, especially during any time of year when the water was too low for boats and conditions got rainy and muddy. In 1922, county officials made plans to cut a sixty-foot roadway along our south line, eastward to the Black Oak Road which ran north and south three-and-a-half miles away. At that time, the first half mile east of us was solid woodland, and only sporadic attempts at clearing had been made in scattered areas beyond.

It was in these partially cleared sections that work began in August of that year. Will was made overseer of the road crew, in charge of about twenty-five Negroes who were "working out" their annual poll taxes. Three days' labor was required of each man, and most people elected to pay

52

such taxes this way, in order to save as much sorely-needed cash as possible. Labor was cheap, but a dollar in cash was hard to come by. On the same day that Will and his crew started work, the Haversticks, using the same sort of so-called "free" road labor, began cutting out the roadway along their south line to join up with us on the west.

The Barhams and Graftons, as I've mentioned, cut out the densely-wooded half mile of roadway due east of us, for which they were paid the munificent sum of $60. They really earned it, but considered themselves lucky to have a paying job during the slack farming season.

That fall was a busy and eventful one for us, despite the lean harvest. Will and I put the finishing touches on our fourth house, and then went to work cutting timber for John Haverstick.

It was also that fall that John's uncle, old Jim Haverstick, died of chest cancer. Uncle Jim (he was "uncle" to all of us, as was John's father, Uncle George) was a homely, deep-voiced old fellow, gruff but quite accommodating. He was almost seventy when he died, and despite the nature of his illness, was "working in the traces" until the very last. On the night he died, he had taken a load of cotton to town and remained overnight to help with a grandson who was seriously ill with pneumonia. In the night Uncle Jim suffered a hemorrhage, and when his daughter became hysterical on seeing blood gush from his mouth, the old man showed his mettle. "What do you want to get all excited for?" he said. "If my time has come, just let me go."

His body was taken back to Indiana for burial, and while the family was away attending the funeral, Will stayed at their place, weighing cotton for the Negro pickers, overseeing the hauling of cotton to town, and taking care of other chores.

Meanwhile, our sharecroppers were busy harvesting the meager result of their year's hard work and growing daily more discouraged. Just before harvest time, there had been some trouble between Lee Grafton and his half-brother

53

Vernon, after which Lee carried a revolver around with him. Soon he sold out his share and went back to Mississippi. When the others had finished gathering their small crop of corn and cotton, they, too, packed up and moved back to Hattiesburg.

We were sorry to lose them and sorry, too, that they had not fared better. After our own earlier experiences in cultivating stumpy, root-filled new ground, we could readily appreciate how the expression, "a hard row of stumps," originated. Our renters had learned from the same harsh teacher, who also applied the boll weevil lash to them.

Ironically, the boll weevil had been largely responsible for their leaving Mississippi originally. Like thousands of others from the Deep South, they had trekked toward a Promised Land — not so much in search of something, like the Forty-Niners of gold-rush days, but to get away from something. Yet the boll weevil, having fattened on the cotton of the Deep South, had moved northward faster than our people in their covered wagons, and was lying in wait for them when they arrived. "The boll weevil — which is a bug long years ago — robbed people of their homes," said Huddie Ledbetter in the preface to his song about the terrible beetle. That says it as succinctly as I know, except that, for the farmers of Arkansas, the boll weevil is hardly a thing of the past. This "bug long years ago" still comes along now and then to eat up everything a man has worked for all year long.

Another Mississippian who had come into our section earlier to escape the boll weevil was a big bear of a man named Cooper. He had bought a plantation on the St. Francis River north of us. In a puckish vein he named it Boll Weevil Plantation, and he soon found out what a fitting name it was.

Because of his tremendous size, he was known as Big Cooper, or sometimes Whispering Cooper, in humorous reference to his powerful voice. He was usually good-natured, but sometimes got down in the dumps and would

54

sit out on his front porch beside the river and twang out sad blues songs on his battered old guitar. Directly across the river lived a woman who was almost as big and fat as Cooper was. One evening, between spells of guitar playing, he called over to her in his booming voice, "Are you ever a-going to git married?"

"I would if I could find anyone that'd have me," she answered back.

"Well," boomed out Cooper, "swim this here river and I'll have you."

They were married not long afterwards. I like to think she swam the river. At any rate, she got across.

VII BOOTS AND BOATS:

Some Observations That Are All Wet

It was said, quite truthfully, that the two things necessary in the Arkansas lowlands were boots and boats. But each had first claim — you needed a boat to get the boots, and boots to get to the boat. It was a toss-up, perhaps best solved by buying your boots before the fall rains set in.

Through the fall and winter, men all wore hip boots, but under normal conditions — meaning anything short of a full-fledged gilt-edged barn-floating flood — the tops were turned down to knee length, using a distinctive fold that gave them the swashbuckling flair of footwear sported by pirates of old. But I doubt if Captain Kidd and his boys ever put in a hard day's work wearing such boots. The worst problem was the moisture that collected inside the boots when you'd toiled in them all day. At night we sometimes dried them out by stuffing them with heated oats . . . which worked fine if you got all the oats out next morning. Woe to those who missed a searing grain or two.

During the first fall when we were staying with the

56

Odums, we needed help with land clearing. Old Man Odum needed boots. So we arranged for him and his son Herbert to do some clearing. About two o'clock one afternoon they asked for their money and left. They knew what the boots cost, had earned exactly that much, and preferred to take it and quit rather than work the rest of the day and have a little extra spending money. Soon Herbert needed new hip boots, too, and we hired them again. This time they had earned enough by noon on the second day to pay for the boots. Immediately they stopped for their pay and left.

In the rainy season from late November to April, what few roads we had ceased to exist as transportation arteries. Boats became our primary link with the outside world.

Several packet boats steamed regularly up and down the St. Francis, making scheduled trips into town, as I recall, on Wednesdays and Saturdays and extra runs if business justified them. Saturday was of course the big day, when Marked Tree really came to life with farmers, lumbermen, river rats, and sharecroppers all flocking in to do the week's shopping, have "co-cola" at the Arkansas Drug, swap stories, watch each other stroll up and down the street, and, not infrequently, raise cain.

The best known of all the boats on the St. Francis, perhaps the most famous in the whole state, was *The Ozark*, owned by Uncle Charlie Cummins, most redoubtable of all rivermen in that country before he mellowed with age. The heyday of Uncle Charlie and *The Ozark* was almost over when we first settled in Arkansas, although the beautiful old boat still made regular runs on the St. Francis.

More prominent steamers in our time were Ned Holman's *Lone Star* and the *Kate,* owned by Old Man Kline. The *Lone Star* was a side-wheeler, while *Kate* was stern propelled. About 1924, after several years of service, the *Lone Star* went down a few miles above Luttrell's Landing. No effort was made to float her, and for a number of years, I'm told, her watery grave was marked by parts of her upper deck jutting above the surface.

Another boat was the *Jim Lee,* named for its owner. Captain Jim was known for his bouts with John Barleycorn, which he frequently lost. Once he passed out too close to an open fire and burned off his leg — a wooden one, fortunately, which he fastened on with leather straps, his own leg having been amputated just below the knee. On another festive occasion, he took the peg-leg off and laid it aside, whereupon a Negro cook, thinking it was firewood, poked it into the galley range. Fortunately, such legs were easily come by where timber was so plentiful. Jim whittled himself another one.

Once he brought a load of hay and other supplies down the slough to our house and stayed overnight. He liked to play the fiddle, and that night before going to bed in the room upstairs, he sawed away for an hour or two, pounding loudly on the floor with his peg-leg in time with the music. Later we noticed big dents in the soft wooden floor — a permanent reminder of Jim's visit.

The larger river boats added to their capacity by pushing a barge ahead of them. This was where the male passengers rode, standing or sitting on the edges, wind-blown and half-chilled. The steamer's small cabin space was reserved for what few women might be on board.

Making landings with a barge was ticklish business. Upstream landings could be made by simply heading the barge directly into shore, but if the boat and barge were headed downstream, a full turn had to be made, so that the upper end of the barge could be pushed alongside the shore. There were no real wharves, the shoreline itself serving as a dock.

Like the local trains, the boats shuttled around casually and with little regard for schedules. Passengers learned to expect almost anything. Once we were heading upstream on the *Kate* when Cap'n Kline grabbed up his shotgun and banged away at a duck flying overhead. When it fell into the river behind us, he reversed engines and we chugged downstream in fits and starts until the bird could be recovered. Another time two girls created quite a furor as the boat was attempting to land. They were apparently arguing over a boy, and the discussion grew so heated that one girl whipped out a knife and was about to whittle a few licks on her opponent when other passengers managed to dissuade her and restore peace.

Coming home on the river, we usually got off the boat at Luttrell's Landing, about nine miles by water below Marked Tree. Here the river makes a U-turn and flows back north about a mile before turning south again, and here also Big Broadmouth slough opens out of the St. Francis and cuts across to the southwest some four or five miles before rejoining the river downstream. At Luttrell's Landing, Big Broadmouth is, despite its name, quite narrow — no more than fifty feet across. It rapidly widens, however, and for most of its length maintains a fairly constant width of about five hundred feet, occasionally reaching eight hundred feet and resembling in outline a curved, elongated toy balloon, firmly inflated except for the short narrow mouthpiece and a slender "nipple" at the end where it empties back into the St. Francis.

If we got off the boat at Luttrell's Landing, we walked a short cut of slightly over two miles, some distance from Big Broadmouth, to our house. But whenever we had a load of supplies too heavy to carry on foot, we rode the boat on down to the lower end of Broadmouth, eight miles or so beyond Luttrell's Landing as one follows the course of the winding river. From here it was only about a mile and a half back up Big Broadmouth to our place, over ground that a wagon and team could get across more easily than the trail to Luttrell's.

This was where I got off Kline's boat one afternoon with a load of hay I'd bought in town. Will had driven the wagon down to the river from the farm, tied the mules, and walked back home, not knowing when I might arrive on the erratic boat run.

Kline was in unusually high spirits, for I was his last

passenger on the trip. As we unloaded the hay, he extended his bottle and offered me a drink. I didn't care for it, but to avoid offending him, I took three or four swallows, assuming a cheerful mien. I didn't have to assume very long; the effect was almost instantaneous. By the time Kline chugged off and left me loading the hay into the wagon, I was giving some serious thought to simply flapping my wings and flying home. I managed to restrain myself, however, and finally got the hay in the wagon, piled three bales high. I had no way to tie it down, and simply perched myself atop the swaying bales and hung on for dear life as the wagon bounced and lurched up the slough. Through some miracle my inebriated zigs somehow coincided with the wagon's zags, and the trusty mules got me home without serious mishap. Will and Frank Walters, who was share-cropping for us at the time, watched me suspiciously as we unloaded the wagon, but I offered no explanations. But it was too late, of course; I should have kept my mouth shut down on the river.

On another occasion, I got off the boat at Luttrell's Landing with John Haverstick and one of his hired hands, a young fellow named Parker Hood. We started down the Haverstick side of the slough, but it had just rained and the slough waters had spread across the low ground there. John and Parker were wearing hip boots and so were prepared, but for some reason or another, I had left my boots behind. When we reached the first wide stretch of water, Parker offered to carry me piggy-back, and I accepted. Soon we came to more water, and since my feet were still dry, I reluctantly let him carry me again. This continued for perhaps a mile altogether, despite my growing protests. Whenever he grew tired, Parker would set me down on a stump and rest awhile. He was a good-hearted fellow, about whom I shall have more to say later.

But of all the hazards I experienced in ploughing my way around the country in boats and boots, the worst by far was an incident that took place late one fall day when

I got off the boat at Cummins' place about two miles below Luttrell's Landing. We did not often go that way, but getting off there placed me slightly nearer home and meant that I could follow an almost due-south course home. Wearing hip boots and carrying a heavy sack of groceries, I set out confidently, passed a familiar row of houses, then entered the trackless woods as night fell. My plan was to angle slightly east so as to hit Big Broadmouth opposite our place, then have Will bring the boat across for me. But I walked and walked for what seemed like hours, and by the time I reached slough water, I was sure I'd miscalculated and gone too far south, past our house and into Broadmouth Flats where the slough makes a backward curve at its southern end and turns west to rejoin the river.

An icy white moon had risen, and in its faint light I began to follow the slough back north, expecting any minute to stumble onto the clearing where we usually crossed with the skiff. It was hard going in the swampy low ground, and by now I was almost exhausted. Minutes that seemed like hours passed, step followed squishy step in the mucky gumbo, and still no clearing, no tell-tale lamp glow from where our house ought to be, not a single familiar landmark that I could identify in the cold moonlight. Then I heard river water just ahead of me, rushing through the narrow neck of the slough, and I realized that I was approaching Luttrell's Landing, at least three miles north of where I thought I was. In the woods I had angled back east too soon and struck Broadmouth *above* our place rather than below it, then had compounded my error by heading back upstream. I was only a few hundred yards from where I'd gotten off the boat.

Remembering the houses I'd passed earlier, I headed back toward them, passing along the way wooden skeletons of two houses just being built, desolate and spectral under the moon's cold beams. When I reached the row of inhabited dwellings, all were dark except the last one, a small two-room shack from which shone a most welcome light. I knocked and was invited in, although I was a complete stranger and must have been quite a bedraggled sight.

The tiny house was occupied by an elderly couple, their son, daughter-in-law, and two small grandchildren. I was bone weary after my long hike with the heavy pack of groceries, too tired even to worry about my empty, growling stomach (for I'd had no supper). When the old couple invited me to spend the night, I readily accepted, although there were but two beds for the seven of us, both in the same small room, which also doubled as the living room.

I could scarcely keep my eyes open, but an hour or two passed and they made no move toward going to bed, and I couldn't figure out any way of retiring gracefully in their presence. The awkward situation may have deterred them, too, or perhaps they felt they must show their hospitality by entertaining me. I finally learned that I was to sleep with grandpa, but it seemed an eternity before he sat down on one of the beds, shucked his pants, and was covered up in an instant. That was my cue. I went to the far side and followed his example. I never knew what sleeping arrangements the others made, for in a second I was dead to the world.

As one might imagine, rivers and boats have played a significant role in the history of Marked Tree. The town in fact owes its name to its unique location on the banks of two rivers — the St. Francis and the Little — and the effect this had on early river travel.

It all came about because the Little River, in its generally southwestern course down to the St. Francis, extends to within a quarter-mile of the larger river, then suddenly bends back north, like a cobra rearing its head, and runs more or less parallel, but in an opposite direction, to the St. Francis before finally emptying into it a mile or so above

Marked Tree. The St. Francis flows through several of its own bends as it comes down past the town, making it possible for an early wit to write that "Marked Tree is twice located upon the Little River and three times located on the St. Francis" — no mean feat for a burg whose population at the time could not have exceeded two thousand.

In the last century, Indians and early settlers in the area discovered the peculiar juxtaposition of the two rivers and found that in traveling upstream they could save several miles of hard paddling by portaging across at one point where the channels curve to within a few hundred yards of each other. To identify this portage place, they marked a tree on the east bank of the St. Francis (according to one tradition, the tree was marked by the Murrell outlaw gang that terrorized Tennessee and eastern Arkansas in the early 1800's). The town had its beginnings in the 1880's, when a railroad was laid through the region and a camp for workers established "at the marked tree." Thus the town was given its unusual name. The original marked tree apparently survived until 1890, when during a storm it was struck by lightning, caved into the river, and was washed away. The place where it stood is still proudly pointed out to visitors — just why I don't know, for the location is now occupied by a broken-down cotton gin that looks as if it too might cave into the river any minute.

The numerous bends of the St. Francis and Little Rivers around Marked Tree are responsible for a story, probably apocryphal but quite possible, that local residents love to tell. It seems that two fellows, many years ago, went exploring down a river in a small boat. They came to a settlement, inquired its name, and were told they had arrived at Marked Tree. They resumed their journey and had gone on downstream through crooks and curves about three miles when they came to another town and asked where they were.

"Marked Tree," a native told them. They went on, and after bending and twisting through another two miles or so, again reached a populated area, repeated the same inquiry, and got the same reply: Marked Tree. One of the poor fellows was reportedly so vexed that he cried out, "I'll give fifty dollars to anyone who can get us away from this damned place." Other people, not traveling on the river, have been known to utter similar sentiments.

VIII THE TREES FELL:

View From One End of
a Crosscut Saw

Although the woods on our Arkansas farm had been cut over at one time, long years before we came, a great deal of salable timber had grown up in the intervening years. As circumstances permitted, we attempted to harvest it and found ourselves increasingly involved in logging operations.

We hired as much help as possible, particularly during the first year or two, despite the difficulty in finding reliable workers. Mr. Keth was the best lumberjack we ever knew, and even he was not immune to the call of the wild. Local inhabitants showed a marked tendency to lose their zest for labor whenever the fish were biting or a fresh batch had cooked off in the moonshine still. We were constantly amazed at the stories they invented and the ingenious methods they devised to escape work.

A Negro lad working for us learned that I was a receptive audience and would engage in long, rambling conversations that gave him an opportunity to pause and lean on the saw.

Between spells of sawing one day he announced, "I'se goan git married this fall." It seemed to be all settled, but then, after a long pause, he blinked and added vacantly, "If I can find a gal make me a good wife."

One year we hired a white man and a Negro to saw down some oak, for which we were to pay them each about $1.75 per day, and furnish their lunch. As the noon hour neared every day we would notice a flurry of activity in the woods, and on the dot of twelve — or even a few minutes after — a tree would come crashing down. Then our woodmen would appear, hungry and looking as if they'd just cut down the Great Redwood Forest. The same thing would happen at quitting time in the afternoon — a tree brought down just as the "shift" ended. For a while we were quite impressed by the way they worked right up to the minute, rather than finding excuses to quit early, as so many did. Then we began to notice the number of trees they cut — or rather, the number they didn't cut — and it became apparent that after cutting one or two, they would start another, loaf awhile, and then bring it toppling down impressively just at quitting time.

Still, we lacked proof and were reluctant to accuse them of malingering. Both were burly rascals and we had learned to respect the fiery temperament of our backwoods neighbors. Even if the charges were true, they might not accept them generously. So, whenever they were not around, I would take some chalk and tally their daily output by marking the trees they had felled on a given day. Soon we knew they weren't doing much, and they knew we knew. The frontier code demanded that they quit, without a word passing between us about their shiftlessness.

While the two men were working for us, we fed them their lunch, as I've mentioned. The Negro had separate but equal eats out on the porch, while we and the white man dined more regally, sitting on home-made benches at the home-made table. Will and I would actually have preferred the Negro to the worthless white man, who would work genially enough with the Negro but not eat with him, which, according to local custom, would be demeaning.

During our first winter in the woods, we cut off several thousand board feet of timber. We were paid ten dollars per thousand feet for hackberry and gum logs, eleven dollars per thousand for elm logs, and fifteen dollars per thousand for stove-size ash. If the ash were twelve inches or more in diameter at the small end, it brought twenty-five dollars per thousand. We also cut and sold one hundred and sixteen elm binders, used in rafting logs together, for which we got twenty cents apiece.

Our first "crop" of two hundred and twenty-four logs scaled 11,180 feet and brought a hundred and fifty-six dollars. Later we cut and sold enough to bring the total to two hundred and seventy-five dollars for the entire season.

The following winter of 1920-21 we were able to log off much more and got good prices. In October, 1920, Will wrote enthusiastically to our folks that we had "managed to get a contract for 150,000 feet of timber at the old prices before the slump came." A timber scale later showed that we fell slightly short of the contract, getting out only 104,000 feet, at an average price of about twenty-four dollars per thousand. Will's letter reported on some of our expenses: "We pay Haversticks $7.50 per thousand for hauling to Big Broadmouth and are hiring the cutting done which, with what work we do ourselves, costs about $2.75 a thousand. We pay the cutters $4 a day and board."

As in the previous year, John Haverstick had contracted to haul our felled logs to the slough, where they could later be rafted and floated down to the St. Francis and from there to the mills down-river. This hauling work benefited a number of interests. John's wagons and teams, which otherwise would have been idle, were specially fitted for this kind of work, and he had a ready labor market in his Negro sharecroppers, who were anxious to have steady work and get extra cash at a time when there was little farm work for them to do.

Each wagon was pulled by four or five mules — two or three leaders and two wheel-mules. During the height of our operations in 1920-21, Haversticks were using four "five-up" teams and hauling out more than 20,000 feet a day.

The mules had my sympathy. The logging trails were rough and rutted, and whenever a heavily-loaded wagon was stopped by a chuck hole, the driver would lash the mules mercilessly instead of getting down to dig out in front of the wheel or chunk up the hole. Finally, with almost super-mule effort, the animals would get the load moving again. Later John hired a repairman to keep the longer, more frequently-used logging roads in shape, and the mule-lashing diminished.

These wagons were usually driven by Negroes, although whites were also employed. The driver always rode the left wheel-mule, holding the lines in his left hand and the whip in his right, so that he had ready access to any laggard mule who required the lash. As I've indicated, few drivers spared the whip. It is interesting to note that the famous Conestoga wagons used to transport early pioneers and their goods were driven by a man riding the left rear horse, passing other wagons on the left. It was this habit which resulted in automobile drivers occupying the lefthand seat.

The logs were hauled to a dump on Big Broadmouth just below our first two houses. For several years, even before we bought the place, Haversticks had used part of our frontage and theirs just below it as a log dump. One summer when the slough was dry, they had cleared out brush in the channel bed to form a floatroad some thirty feet wide and running from the log dump down to the lower end of Broadmouth. Sometime during each winter, water would rise high enough in the slough so that we could raft the logs and float them down to the river. However, the St. Francis had to be running high up above before water would be diverted into Big Broadmouth at its narrow upper end, and we always hoped for plenty of rain whenever rafting was to be done. That year we had it in abundance. At

68

Memphis the weather record for the first four months of 1921 showed 31.46 inches, almost thirteen inches above normal. By the middle of March we had rafted out three-fourths of the crop.

Time was always a crucial element in these operations. We could not begin cutting before a given date in the fall, set by the lumber companies each year when they were satisfied that the timber beetle season had passed; but it was to our advantage to cut the trees as soon after the date as possible, since we rafted our lumber to the mill and wanted the cut logs, especially oak, to lighten by "drawing." This could be accomplished by felling the trees and leaving them untrimmed for as long as possible before winter weather set in, so that the withering leaves would draw sustenance from the trunks and thus lighten them. But as a result, we were always "in a bind" between the lumber companies' logging date and the onset of bad weather. The cutting period also had to coincide with high water, so that we could get the logs rafted and not leave them in the dump too long.

As I've indicated, things went rather smoothly that winter of 1920-21. Rafting got underway on schedule, with John and Will making up the rafts while I snaked elm binders out of the woods with a mule. The binders were placed parallel to the stream, then the logs, one by one, were pushed underneath, crosswise to the binders, and fastened in place with rafting spikes. Two binders were usually required — one at each end of the logs — but some rafts were made up with only one binder at the center. Cant hooks, peaveys, and spike poles were used in the work.

In making up the rafts we had to use great care in sorting the logs so that "floaters" and "sinkers" struck a balance. Green oak, of course, sinks, and although we tried to intersperse it with floaters of maple and ash, such light woods were none too plentiful. The size of the squared rafting spikes was also important in making a buoyant raft. A collection of these spikes, the only one I've ever seen, is at Knott's Berry Farm near Los Angeles. Some of our rafts

69

went to the mill like icebergs — about nine-tenths under water. There was the ever-present danger that they would bob a time or two and vanish altogether, although we never quite lost one.

Getting the rafts to the river could be dangerous, but I found it most exciting. Long spike or rafting poles were used to keep the rafts from snagging brush or running aground on bends, and raft jockeys needed agile feet to keep themselves and the raft balanced. On one of my first rafting trips, we hit the swift current in lower Broadmouth unexpectedly, and the front of the raft went down like the Lusitania. We managed to save it and ourselves only by jumping quickly to the back end and achieving a precarious balance for a few minutes until the raft could be brought under control.

Landing and securing such a raft is hardly child's play, either. A hundred-ton block of logs can exert tremendous force in swift water, and it takes a lot of know-how and experience to stop one. They are best anchored by degrees, keeping the tie-rope slack at first and tightening it slowly. I've seen, much to my surprise, tie-ropes almost two inches thick snap apart when tightened too fast to an anchoring tree. Even a slow-moving raft has an awesome forward thrust one would never suspect.

Our part in the operation was over when the timber reached the river, where more experienced mill-hands took charge of the rafts and herded them to the sawmills downstream.

Old-time loggers told of a phenomenal timber thief who cut loose an anchored raft and sold it to the nearest sawmill downstream, then went back that night, cut it loose again, sold it to a mill farther on, cut it loose again — well, they made a longer story of it, but I think we'd soon run out of mills.

Although we did not quite fill the 150,000-feet contract that winter of 1920-21, our timber crop grossed about $2,500.

70

This was more than double the amount we got in any other single year.

In the fall of 1921, we hired Uncle Jap (Jasper) Leatherwood and his son, Brack, to hew out railroad ties. The Leatherwoods lived on high dry ground at the lower end of Big Broadmouth, near the point where it empties back into the St. Francis. Their location was slightly less isolated than most outposts in the wilderness, being a sort of crossing place for traffic from both the river and the slough. There they farmed a few acres of rich cotton ground, enjoyed unusually good fishing, took life easy, and never interfered with the business of their neighbors.

Uncle Jap was a great jovial fat man who paddled around in his homemade dugout canoe, looking like some wise old river god in his ceremonial barge. On several occasions he ferried me across the slough with the dugout riding so low in the water that waves lapped over the stern. I held my breath but Uncle Jap was a real riverman and didn't seem to mind it a bit. If the boat had sunk, he would no doubt have floated high.

It was rumored that he and Brack ran a secret still in the low Broadmouth Flats back of their house, but no one ever knew positively. Cutting railroad ties for us that fall was probably the most strenuous work they ever did, for no one was so well-adjusted to the easy-come, easy-go aspects of backwoods life as Uncle Jap and Brack.

In cutting ties, oak logs are sawed into 8½-foot lengths, then hewn up into ties 6 x 8 inches or 7 x 9 inches. Either size is almost too heavy for one man to lift and carry very far, as I learned at the expense of a sore back. Since we had employed several others in addition to the Leatherwoods, Will and I working together usually attended to the business of loading and unloading. We cut approximately 700 ties that fall, and netted about 20¢ apiece on them.

Later that winter we put out about 15,000 feet of ash at $23 per thousand feet for No. 1 grade and twelve dollars per thousand for No. 2. Not much of it was top-grade.

71

In 1922, with all of our farm rented out to the Barhams and Graftons, Will and I contracted to cut timber for John Haverstick at $1.50 per 1000 feet. We felled a total of 1,243 trees for John that season, and prided ourselves on cutting 1,043 before accidentally throwing one into another tree and lodging it. Then we seemed jinxed and lodged six or eight more before reaching our grand total.

Getting a lodged tree down was quite dangerous. Without warning, the supporting tree might split up violently while being sawed, and even if it didn't, the direction of fall was difficult to gauge.

One day we inadvertently threw a falling tree on a stray cow. We thought little about it after she got up right away and began browsing on leaves, but the next morning we found her dead. We were not liable for damages, however, for there was in effect a stock law, something rather new at that time. Only a few years earlier, the law of open range had prevailed, and any land owner who wanted his property and crops protected from cattle had to fence them out. Now it was the stock owner's responsibility to keep them fenced in. The poor cow had strayed where she had no business and, legally, was guilty of trespassing.

It is strange, but falling trees seem to have an attraction for ranging cattle; I've often seen them gathered around a freshly-felled log, munching the leaves as if no others existed, when all the time they're surrounded by a dense undergrowth of bushes.

Most of the trees we cut for John were sweet gums, which exhibit several interesting characteristics. If one of these trees has been slashed with an axe or otherwise had its bark broken, a thick, sticky substance seeps out around the wound, forming a gum that many people like to chew.

Sometimes when sawing down a sweet gum we would hear the sudden hiss of escaping gas, which accumulates whenever there is a hollow in the tree. This gas is inflammable, and we occasionally relieved the tedium of our work by sticking lighted matches to the gas pockets.

72

After logging for the Haversticks, we cut 458 trees on our own place that winter of 1922-23. These grossed slightly over $1,000, making that our second best timber year.

The next winter, that of 1923-24, we got out slightly over 50,000 feet which sold at $17.50 per 1000 and grossed almost $900. After that our logging operations declined into a rather hit-and-miss affair. Prices were unstable and we seemed to have cut most of the prime timber. Yet there were plenty of trees left standing; the farm was not completely cleared until more than twenty years after we bought it.

IX   MAN AND BEAST

Wildlife in
"All Righten Country"

I feel an urge to gush a little here and begin this section with something warm and poetic, perhaps such as this: "Despite the rigors and hardships of the remote frontier, our lives were daily enriched by the friendly animals of the field and wood who gambolled at our door, the gay birds who chattered through the timberlands, the myriad fauna that inhabited our rustic, wooded homeland." That would no doubt please the Wednesday Afternoon Society of Tea Sippers, Book Lovers, and Beagle Fanciers, as well as any others who tend to take a romantic view of the relationship between man and beast. It is also for the most part true enough. But the slant is all wrong, and I shall resist the temptation to wax eloquent over mules, ducks, bears, turkeys, snakes, chickens, hogs, and such.

It was simple enough: the animals were there, and so were we. We tried to get on friendly terms with those that were domesticated or could be tamed, forming a sort of tacit non-aggression pact with them, just as in the case of

74

our more amenable human neighbors. The wild ones of both species we appreciated for their spirit and style, but we tried to keep them at a respectful distance, and interfered with them as little as possible. "Nature teaches beasts to know their friends," according to Shakespeare.

Our greatest affection was for the mules, Sam and Rhoda, but this I suppose, was based largely on our compatible personalities. Sam and "Rhody" were among our first acquisitions in Arkansas, and we never made a better investment. (Despite Rhody's feminine name, they were both "horse" mules — the closest thing to manhood a mule can get.)

They were not too well matched according to size, Sam being smaller and built closer to the ground, but they teamed together as well as those big log-wagon mules of John Haverstick's — sometimes even better. Only rarely did Sam's diminutive size prove a handicap. One such occasion was when I tried to drive the wagon across Little Broadmouth slough, hauling at least a hundred pounds of groceries. I coaxed Sam and Rhody down the steep bank into the channel bed, whereupon both mules promptly went down in the mud at the bottom. I managed to get the team unhitched, and Rhody slogged out, but poor old Sam remained stuck, his hind legs in the mire up to his belly. Although the water was rather shallow, there was enough to drown the struggling mule if he tired and lay over, as he seemed likely to do. I ran to get a rope so Rhody could pull him out, but when I returned with help, Sam had vanished — but into the barn, where I later found him, rather than into the sloughbed. He'd given up too soon in the mud, after the fashion of many a mule. While I was gone for help, he'd apparently grown determined, another common mule-trait, and pulled himself out. Next day, operating from the bank, Sam and Rhody retrieved the wagon.

In 1922 when we had no crop ourselves, we rented our mules for ten dollars a month to the Barhams and Graftons, who used them during the height of the crop season to supplement their own work animals. At other times when we had no need for them, we let them range wherever they wished. There were no fences to keep them from wandering off to California or Tlaxcala. If a horse were ranging anywhere near, we would likely find them with it, for mules tend to accept horses as leaders. We also looked for them wherever wild cane grew, for they considered it a choice tidbit. On the domestic side, they relished rolled oats and pancakes, as we discovered in experimenting with their gastronomic interests. However, the oats and pancakes tended to stick to their mouths. Our curiosity being satisfied, they got no more of such foods.

We later bought a second team of mules. Although they were satisfactory enough as work animals, they somehow lacked mule-personality, and we never grew as attached to them as to Sam and Rhody.

One year we needed some extra mule power in plowing, and John Haverstick lent us one of his animals, named Jesse. He was a big, powerful fellow who worked beautifully in plowing previously cultivated ground — but when it came to new ground, and all the sudden jolts and stops caused by tree roots, Jesse decided he had had enough. He literally balked like a mule. For a time we tried whipping him. He would start on, but the balks became more and more frequent, the starts increasingly more reluctant, the lickings less and less effective. Finally, we conceded defeat and gave up trying to use him.

Jesse had another typical mule habit that made him unwelcome. He kicked. And it was not enough for him to take a random swing or two at somebody passing behind him; he would glance around out of the corner of his shifty eyeballs and try to find somebody to kick. If you were standing off to one side, even out of range, he would wheel his posterior and kick with both feet. I suppose he could have killed you if he struck the right place, but we learned to avoid him.

76

John hadn't intentionally tried to "wish hard luck on us," as he would say, by lending us a mean mule. He was as surprised as we were that Jesse turned out bad; Haversticks' land had been in cultivation several years and they had never used Jesse on new ground. Later, on several occasions, we used John's teams to good advantage in both farming and logging operations. Yet our hearts always belonged to Sam and Rhody.

"Some Homer of the cotton fields should sing the saga of the mule and of his place in the South," wrote William Faulkner in one of his early books. To my knowledge, only one such bard has risen to the challenge — Thad Snow, in his wonderful memoir, *From Missouri*. "Mules are not just mules," Snow said. "Each is an individual, and has character and personality of his own. Some are great-minded and some petty and small-minded, like people. Probably I have utterly forgotten ninety-nine out of a hundred people whom I've known. Not so with the mules." At any rate, they are, as Snow wrote, "a vanishing race of noble animals." Just the other day, I noticed in the paper that there are only five mules left in all of Callaway County, Missouri, once considered the mule capital of the world. This is quite a comedown from the county's high of 25,000 mules just after World War I, about the time we were getting acquainted with Sam and Rhody.

As a Christmas present our first year on the farm, our folks in Ohio sent us a collie dog. Poor Sport was destined to have an adventuresome but all-too-brief life in Arkansas. He came to Marked Tree by railway express and promptly "broke jail" while waiting in the express room for me to pick him up. When I arrived in town, he was making a tour of the city, with the express agent hot on his trail. We finally found him, and I headed for the boatlanding with Sport under one arm and a load of groceries in the other. The boat was already pulling out as I reached the bank, and I handed Sport, who wore a collar and short cord, to Uncle George Haverstick, to hold until I could leap aboard the moving boat. Uncle George had no sooner taken the cord and set the dog down on the bank when Sport slipped the collar and bounded off. I was caught in something of a mid-air dilemma, poised awkwardly in the water trying to decide whether to catch the boat or the dog. Uncle George showed greater presence of mind, and instead of spooking the dog by chasing him, simply waited a second or two until Sport stopped of his own volition to sniff out his new surroundings. Then he grabbed up the delinquent canine and heaved him out to the departing boat, just as I tackled it and climbed aboard with the sack of groceries.

Our cat, Evangeline, did not take kindly to Sport at first, but later seemed to acquire unusual affection for him, as not infrequently occurs when natural enemies have to live together and get to know each other. Soon, whenever the cat saw Sport lying on the floor, she would crawl up on him and stretch out. Sport was not too thrilled at being used for a bed by this strange, purring animal, but she forcefully insisted on her rights even when he tried to shove her away. Their friendship had hardly ripened when Sport died of black-tongue a few weeks after that disastrous day in March, 1920, when Will almost cut off his foot and Mr. Keth and I ruined the new crosscut saw.

A year or so later we got another dog but had even worse luck with him. After running with a neighbor's dogs, which we later learned had been exposed to hydrophobia, our dog began to have momentary fits of violence. Finally he threatened to attack Will and me as we were trying to tie him up, and Will had to shoot him. All this sounds quite tame, but it was one of the most harrowing experiences I've ever gone through. The dog had bared his teeth rather hideously and was growling like the mad beast he must have been. He lunged at us several times before I could get the gun, and I think he was deterred from ripping into us only because Will and I were so scared that we were acting even crazier than he was. Our belief that the dog had rabies was supported by two doctors in Marked Tree, but the veterinarian held that it was enteritis, an equally fatal disease, which he said is often mistaken for hydrophobia. We were told that mules suffering from enteritis had been known to kill humans.

After the dog's demise and that of Evangeline, our sole pet was a big yellow cat named Nip, who daily followed us back and forth from the house to the field and earned his name from nipping at our bare feet whenever we took our boots off. He also had a feline habit of running into the woods ahead of us as we walked along, then pouncing out like some ferocious but comically stunted tiger. Backwoods life was lonely for animals as well as for humans, and we all played our trivial, private little games to ease the boredom.

Among the first farm animals to join our menagerie were seven young pigs, obtained as a sort of portable pork supply, the idea being that we could butcher them off as needed. Rising meat prices, however, induced us to sell four of them to a meat market in town, which paid us eleven cents a pound for the porkers, dressed and delivered. The other three eventually wound up on our table.

In 1923 we bought four hogs from a man across the St. Francis, who agreed to keep them until we could come for them. Late in December Mr. Keth and I rowed our flat-bottomed john boat down Big Broadmouth to the river, then back north past Leatherwoods' about a mile upstream and over to the west bank where the owner of the hogs lived. He had everything ready for us, and with his help, we butchered the four pigs on the spot and brought the carcasses back in the boat.

Hog-butchering is a lost art on most farms today, but it was something of an event back then, and we prided ourselves on a neat, clean job. Mr. Keth shot the four hogs, then "stuck" them, using a long knife to open the jugular vein and empty as much blood as possible from the body. "Bleeding like a stuck hog" is an apt figure; the thick red fluid gushes out in a seemingly endless stream.

Next we placed each hog, one at a time, on boards and covered it with cloth sacks, then poured boiling water over it so that the hair could be scraped off. Then we put a stick through the tendons of the back legs and swung the animal up on a pole stretched between two trees. This enabled us to finish the scraping and slit the belly to remove the entrails and other parts. After the animals had hung for awhile and drained out thoroughly, we put them in the boat and headed home, where we finished the job by cutting up the hams, sides, and shoulders, then salting the meat down to preserve it. All this was not easily accomplished, but it had saved the greater difficulties of driving and boating the hogs home alive.

In February, 1920, we made our first plunge into the poultry business with eight Plymouth Rock hens and a rooster purchased from a woman in Marked Tree. For these we paid twenty-one cents a pound, a total of $10.15. One hen suffocated as I carried them in a sack through town to the boatlanding, but I turned a quick profit by selling it to a restaurant owner for $1.25, slightly more than I had just paid for it.

The chickens flourished on the farm, feeding on bugs and worms, which were plentiful in the new ground. During one nine-day period we got fifty-one eggs from six of the hens (the other one was setting). After six weeks we had sold ten dollars worth of eggs and meanwhile had all we could use ourselves.

One night we found a possum on the chicken roosts we had put up in an open shed. The chickens were squawking and thrashing about, but none of them had been harmed when Will and I investigated. Will was all for killing the possum, but the poor creature's look of innocence and my pleadings prevailed, and finally Will took him away by the tail to a persimmon tree, several hundred yards distant, which was loaded with ripe fruit. Any self-respecting possum ought to prefer ripe persimmons to chicken, but this one failed to take the hint. The next night it was back among the hens — briefly. This time my pleas were in vain. Old Br'er Possum had forfeited his chance to reform.

The next year, when Frank Walters was sharecropping for us, we arranged for Frank and his wife to take care of the chickens. They were to get half of any chicks that hatched and we furnished feed for the other half. A hundred hatched, but five were killed by a possum.

The Swank-Walters Chicken Partnership lasted only one season. Our only other excursion into chicken raising came two years later when Will bought seventeen, induced by high egg prices — up to fifty cents a dozen. Such high profits, however, were short-lived, and so were Will's chickens.

In 1923 we got three settings of duck eggs and borrowed three hens from a sharecropper to set on them. Sixteen hatched, but only five — all drakes — survived the summer. The old mother hen, although somewhat puzzled over her strange offspring, did her best to fulfill her maternal responsibilities, but the ducklings paid her little heed. They took to the water at the first opportunity, despite her worried cluckings, and showed slight interest in the choice tidbits she scratched up for them, preferring to supplement the fruits of their own foraging with corn we fed them out of our hands. As they grew older they would even eat upside down when we held them. They liked biscuit, too, and when called would come waddling up to gulp down the stale bread greedily, run to the water to drink, and rush back for more. They were our favorite bird pets and did much to relieve the tedium of the long days.

There were surprisingly few wild ducks in our area, considering the extent of water. This was of little consequence to us, for neither Will nor I did much hunting of any kind. However, I took the gun one day and went out to scout around for anything that might present itself. Crossing the slough and edging along the bank into the woods, I took care to move along as noiselessly and unobtrusively as possible. I had stopped to get my bearings when suddenly, some sixty feet away in the water, there appeared the thrilling sight of a mother duck and her four little offspring. I watched them a long while, unheard and unseen, as they dipped and floated and paddled idly about. I don't know my ducks but assume they were wood ducks, maybe mallards. At any rate they were beautiful. It would have taken a heartless hunter, indeed, to have broken up such an idyllic family scene. Crouching there, undiscovered, until they finally left, I only wished I had brought a camera instead of a gun.

Years later on a freighter far from land, this peaceful, happy bird scene was brought back to mind in contrast to the sight of two small gulls — evidently a pair — huddled closely beside each other on the deck rail in a driving rain — the very picture of misery. A third derelict bird joined them to share their sea of trouble, in which all three most likely perished.

One day while preparing ground for sudan grass among the stumps, I came across a killdeer's nest. Killdeer, from some strange quirk of nature, prefer to nest out in the open where there is little or no natural protection, relying upon the mother bird's skill as an actress to decoy would-be predators. When her nest is approached by humans, she begins to flutter and tumble across the ground, away from the nest, twittering wildly and thrashing as if both wings were broken. We were almost on the nest that morning when Mama Killdeer went into her act, tumbling convulsively toward the startled mules. It was a successful performance. Sam and Rhody froze in their tracks, and out of consideration for the mother bird's gallant defense of her family, we reserved several square feet for the nest. Actually, it was a nest only in the strictest sense, for killdeer make no real nest like other birds, but simply lay their large, speckled eggs on the ground, always arranged with the small, pointed ends together, forming a sort of swollen X. Later, in scything the sudan, we found four more killdeer nests and always left undisturbed a little patch of ground around them.

82

The most plentiful game bird in our part of Arkansas was the wild turkey. Flocks of thirty or forty could be glimpsed momentarily in the thick undergrowth where they liked to feed. Hunting them was an exciting sport, for it took an experienced tracker and a quick shot to bring one down. The meat of the wild turkey is most delicious, which also helps to explain why they were hunted far more than any other game in the area.

During our first fall on the farm, "Doc" Hanna, a friend of ours from Marked Tree, spent a few days with us hunting the birds. He got two, each of which dressed out at about nine pounds. We shared one, cooked to perfection by Mr. Keth, and "Doc" took the other one back to his girl friend in town.

The best hunting time was in the early dawn, when the gobblers are calling to their mates. Sounds seem to travel especially well in the quiet early morning. One spring day just after getting up, I heard a gobbler ribbling away in the distance. I picked up the shotgun and started toward him, covering more than half a mile and edging slowly closer and closer before I caught sight of him in a small clearing. It should have been an easy shot, but as I pulled the trigger he seemed to vanish before my eyes, as mystifyingly as if he were part of a master magician's act. My visions of a turkey dinner vanished, too.

Despite the rather large turkey population, I killed only one wild turkey all the time I was in Arkansas, and it was a hen, which at the time I regretted killing. But we took the bird to Mrs. Walters and she soothed my feelings somewhat by baking the turkey and whipping up a small feast to go with it. We had a fine meal together.

Will's luck at turkey shooting was no better than mine. His single kill was so young and small that it barely made a meal for us and Mr. Keth.

We were so depressed with our luck that when Adam Baser, a distant neighbor, came to our house one rainy fall day and asked if we'd seen any wild turkeys around, we innocently but truthfully said no. Adam had leaned his Winchester shotgun near the door when he came in. He picked up the gun, stepped out on the porch, and immediately brought down a big tom almost seventy feet away, according to my later measurements. He took his turkey and went home without further comment.

Sportsmen from nearby towns occasionally came out in the spring to hunt turkeys, and would sometimes arrive the evening before and stay overnight with us, so as to be on hand when the gobblers and hens started calling to each other in the morning.

These hunters used various kinds of "callers" to imitate the *kouk! kouk!* of the turkey hen and lure the gobblers. But it could be an advantage to imitate a gobbler as well as a hen, for sometimes when a gobbler called for a mate, another tom would hear him and come up to start a fight. I knew of only one fellow — a professional hunter from Jonesboro — who could really fool the birds by gobbling. When he gobbled, he shook his big head like an old tom himself. He could also imitate a squirrel to perfection. I was with him one day in the woods when he went over to a tree and started chattering. A squirrel came down the tree, answering back angrily and advancing lower and lower until the hunter shot it.

This fellow and another professional hunter camped for awhile in 1921 in the house we had built down on our south line. One day we heard they had killed a bear and went to see. We found it laid out on the kitchen floor — a huge black bruin weighing about three hundred and fifty pounds. Shortly afterward, a cub, probably belonging to it, was killed.

The hunters skinned the old bear and made a rug, which in some way was acquired by a neighboring Negro. He apparently valued the tattered pelt highly, for when his house later caught fire, he rushed in and rescued the bear rug, leaving everything else to burn.

When the bear was butchered, we were given a sample

84

of the meat, but it was tough chewing, like coarse, strong beef. I suppose I shouldn't complain, for the gift of bear meat was about the only consideration we got from the Jonesboro hunters, who displayed some record lows in manners and sportsmanship. One of them — I believe it was the one who "gobbled" — strung a line through the trees and fastened to it fish hooks baited with corn, to attract wild turkeys. The two men exhibited about the same type of behavior toward us and never offered any payment in money or game — other than the slice of old bear — for staying long periods in our tenant house and hunting over our land. When they left, I moved one of them with his load of game and equipment in our wagon two and a half miles to the boat landing. It was hard going in the heavy gumbo, and even though I gave the mules frequent rests, they were almost exhausted. I walked most of the way to save the team, but the hunter never budged from his seat. To avoid a scene, I charged him a mere pittance and was grateful to be rid of him.

Other sportsmen were more congenial. Late in the fall of our first year on the farm, a group from Blytheville camped not far from us on the Haverstick place. Will and I were their guests one night for a supper of soup and squirrel, and Will went back another time for a feast of wild turkey. One of the hunters whom Will thought familiar at first, but could not place, turned out to be one of his old comrades-in-arms, a fellow he had known during his days in the Army Air Corps when they were both in ground school at Columbus, Ohio.

These hunters were after big game — bear or deer — but their haul was limited to wild turkeys, a few squirrel, and a bee tree. We helped them take the honey from the tree. There was at least seventy pounds of it, and they generously gave us six or eight pounds. It was of excellent quality and came in quite handy, for the country was then in the grip of a widespread sugar shortage. We did not suffer much from it, thanks to the honey and a fairly large supply of sugar we had on hand when the squeeze began. But consumers in Marked Tree — if they had sugar at all — paid as much as twenty-five cents a pound for it. The cheapest we knew of was that sold by mail by Montgomery Ward at $2.88 for twenty-five pounds, or about eleven-and-a-half cents a pound.

A few months later a neighbor found a bee tree on our place. We helped cut it and divided the honey, about ten pounds altogether. This was the ninth such tree our neighbor had located in a period of a few weeks. The bees were as industrious as they are reputed to be.

Although it was still winter, I often heard a steady humming above me as I walked through the woods. I at first assumed it was bees, but I rarely saw them, and the noise was so loud and steady that I was skeptical. Nevertheless, it was exactly what I'd suspected — thousands and thousands of bees, seldom seen but constantly droning, feeding high on the tiny maple and elm blooms in the tops of the trees. Years later, reading Charles Dudley Warner's account of his wanderings in the North Carolina mountains in *On Horseback*, I was interested to find that he too had been puzzled by what he described as "this loud and continuous humming overhead, almost like the sound of wind in the pine tops," only to learn as I had that the upper branches were alive with bees.

Two years later we cut down another bee tree which netted us a half-gallon of honey after the comb had been extracted. Bee tree robbers were rarely known to leave anything for the bees, and we were no exceptions. I suppose we felt the risks involved entitled us to all the plunder we could get, for mad bees can inflict serious damage. We were lucky in this respect and always managed to get our honey without being discovered, although I once disturbed a nest of yellow jackets while cutting cross-ties and suffered some agony for my clumsiness. When they started stinging, I started running, but they got me thirteen times, mostly on the north end as I ran south.

The area abounded with several smaller varieties of wildlife. There were no foxes or skunks that I know of, but a few mink were trapped from time to time, and coons were everywhere. And of course the rabbit population was immense. They were mostly "swampers," a variety of rabbit considerably larger than our Ohio cottontails. They were also lean and tough at the table, although our cooking may have been at fault. Anyway, we soon gave up our attempts at rabbit stew.

These swampers had a strange habit of whistling whenever they were disturbed. They would jump up and start to run, letting out a shrill wail or a series of short, sharp whistles as they vanished in a flash into the woods. They were the quarterhorses of rabbitdom; a cottontail would have been left at the post in a race with one.

I always felt the squirrels in the area were deprived, for they had no hickory nuts, chestnuts or beech nuts and survived on acorns and pecans. Most of them were the common gray variety, but I once pulled down three flying squirrels while trying to cut away a vine that grew high into a tree. They were a fascinating sight spread out so beautifully in midair. And to my great surprise, one or two of them actually flew upward — not much, of course, but to the extent that in nearing a landing spot on a tree trunk in their downward flight, they turned and spread their tails so as to let the air pressure and their momentum carry them upward a few feet and thus land more slowly on the tree trunk, facing upward. I didn't try to harm them, beyond shaking them out of the tree, but the damage had been done, and we saw no more of them.

Wolves were also in abundance, but they were mostly heard and not seen. Although we grew accustomed to their wavering, mournful howls, I was never quite at ease, especially if they started barking as I was walking through the woods at night. Parker Hood and I got some of our first gray hairs one night when, while walking home along Big Broadmouth, we were surrounded by a pack of them.

Parker had had more experience with them than I had and was used to going everywhere alone through the woods in search of stray cattle, but as the barking grew louder and louder and we seemed on the verge of being devoured, even he began to lose his aplomb. I just kept repeating the old bromide that wolves would never attack a human. Maybe the animals read my mind and were reluctant to spoil my illusions; at any rate, they eventually went away.

The only wolf I ever saw up close was one that belonged to two old-timers who lived in a tent down the slough. They kept the poor wolf chained, evidently to serve as a watch dog. It was a mangy, sad-looking creature. Its owners were hardly more presentable, although one of them frequently sported a necktie, about the only one I ever saw in that area. Apparently this tonsorial touch was for the benefit of a widow who lived nearby, but it had about the effect of a pig with a ribbon on its tail.

I suppose the howling of wolves was more appealing to the tent-dwellers than to me, for they seemed to share the sentiments of an old trapper who said, "Anywheres I can hear the wolves howling at night is all righten country for me." The country was "all righten," but I would have paid somebody two-bits to get rid of the wolves.

X SNAKES AND MOSQUITOES:

The Venomed Stings of Life — and Death

We managed to live on fairly good terms with most of the animals and insects in our part of Arkansas. There were two major exceptions: snakes and mosquitoes.

Our backwoods country would have been a paradise for a zoologist specializing in the study of snakes. A herpetologist would have discovered some ten or twelve varieties of these reptiles, including garter snakes, king snakes, grass snakes, chicken snakes, pilot snakes, rattlesnakes, and water moccasins. The last two were the only really dangerous ones, but all of them were nuisances, despite the fact that they were beneficial in holding down the population of rodents and other pests. The very sight of an elongated reptile slithering through the grass or hanging from a tree is enough to chill the blood of most humans. I think we often killed them out of instinctive revulsion rather than with malice aforethought, and although we sent many of them to snake-heaven, I doubt if we upset the balance of nature too much. The very number of those we killed indicates how plentiful they were.

In 1921 I killed fifty-two and in 1922 I got thirty-four. The number declined somewhat after that. I began to get accustomed to them, I guess, and I became more and more aware of their value as pest-control agents. I usually tried to spare garter snakes, king snakes and grass snakes.

The only ones I never regretted killing were the rattle-snakes. I ran across twelve of them during five and a half years in Arkansas and killed them all. I was always afraid that if I let one get away, I might meet it again under less favorable, and possibly tragic, circumstances. The same was true of the slimy water moccasins, but they were much harder to catch and kill, and for this reason I think we hated them worse than the rattlers. The few we managed to kill were usually the victims of circumstances, like the one Will and I spotted one day in December, a time unusually late in the year for them to be about. This one took to the water, then seemed to decide it was too cold and came out. Will held it with a scythe while I beheaded it with an axe.

My first experience with a rattler came soon after we'd settled in the woods. I was driving the wagon over a logging road when I saw a snake cross ahead of me and disappear into the thick undergrowth. Although I had never seen one, I suspected that this was a rattlesnake, and with more enthusiasm than good sense, I grabbed a stick and went into the woods after it. I lost it several times in the thick bushes — then suddenly there he was, staring me right in the face, coiled and ready to strike. I managed to get him first, but later realized how foolhardy I had been. There is no dodging the swiftness of a rattler's sword-like thrust, and an average one can strike from one-half to two-thirds of his own length, as we later discovered by teasing one with a hoe handle. Will had a method of killing them from a distance which was a great deal safer. He had practiced throwing a hatchet to make it stick in a tree, and he once threw his forester's axe in the same way at a threatening rattler, neatly decapitating the reptile.

I was cultivating corn one summer day in 1921 when suddenly, for no apparent reason, the mule, big Rhody, stopped. I hawed, "Get up," but he wouldn't budge. Rhody was usually a most obedient animal, and I was quite puzzled until I saw a whopping big rattler directly ahead of the mule. After I'd killed it, beating so vigorously I had a sore arm and shoulder for several days, we discovered it had thirteen rattles and was almost fifty-five inches long and seven and a half inches around.

A few years later, however, I encountered one a great deal bigger. It put up the fiercest fight of any snake I ever tangled with and finally died after the strangest act I've ever witnessed in a beast. I had fought this whopper long and hard in dense undergrowth with a brush axe (which has a curved blade running parallel to the handle and is hardly well suited for killing snakes). I finally managed to break his back. He was still threshing about but I knew he couldn't coil or get away from me. Then as I stepped back to catch my breath, the snake, apparently quite deliberately, reached around and bit itself, seeming to put every particle of remaining strength into this final, desperate effort, which continued for several seconds before the snake died. Whether its own venom was the immediate cause of its death I leave to the experts to judge. In Mrs. Frances Trollope's famous travel book, *Domestic Manners of the Americans* (1832), I ran across a similar instance. Mrs. Trollope and others had just killed a copperhead when a farmer came up: "He told us that he had once seen a copperhead snake bite himself to death, from being teased by a stick."

This snake measured almost seventy inches, including

its thirteen rattles and a button. It was ten and a half inches in circumference and tapered only slightly, which is characteristic of poisonous snakes. I regret that we did not weigh it, but by computations using a cylinder of water approximately the same diameter and length, we arrived at a weight of about seventeen pounds. This is on the conservative side, for a rattler's specific gravity is probably somewhat greater than that of water. A moccasin, at any rate, will sink in water. Siah Morris, who was then working for Dr. Baird and living with me in one of our houses, skinned the big rascal to make a snakeskin belt. Such a possession was prized by some of our neighbors, whose taste in this respect I could not share.

It's almost impossible to predict how a rattler will react when he's discovered. Despite what tradition says, they don't always rattle when they're disturbed. The big one Rhody and I found rattled only once and that only after I'd hit him. Also contrary to popular opinion, most of them are not very belligerent. I wouldn't say they are cowards, exactly, but they normally avoid a fight. The standard tactic is to rattle like mad, bluff to the last card, and try to get away. But you can't depend on it. As I've said, some won't rattle at all. In this connection it is interesting to note that very recent studies have produced evidence that rattlesnakes as a species tend to rattle less and less — it seems that somehow in the evolutionary process they've learned that those who rattle simply attract the attention of their worst predator — man — and are thus more likely to be killed as a result. The moral: if you don't want to lose your head, don't wiggle your tail. Some herpetologists think that in time, the snakes' rattlers will become useless appendages or perhaps even cease to exist.

I'd venture that most of the fatalities suffered on both sides as a result of run-ins between rattlers and people are caused by foolish error on the part of either snake or human. I've witnessed several instances in which an individual would hear a rattle in dense brush and immediately head toward it unarmed, with some vague notion of ferreting out the snake. My own ignorance in chasing the rattler into dense undergrowth is a similar example. And the same is true of the snakes themselves. Many of the ones we encountered and killed could have lived long and happy lives if they had only known what modern-day rattlers apparently do and kept quiet. Some of them could have escaped even after being detected, if they hadn't insisted on picking a fight and tried to whip a hoe handle or an axe blade. But of course the snakes have more excuse for being stupid; human beings are supposed to know better. It's a wonder there weren't more cases of snakebite in our area.

Wild, gory tales of those who'd died in the agony of snakebite were abundant, but I knew of only one person who'd been bitten, and he survived. Many people took extreme precautions; Siah Morris always wore leather leggings, which must have been intolerably hot at times.

In early 1922, the Barhams and Graftons were doing clearing work near Little Broadmouth. On a dry slope, under a large log covered with a mass of limbs twisted over it, they uncovered the most remarkable conglomeration of snakes I ever saw or heard about.

The workers set fire to the brush pile, then noticed the snakes and called to Will and me to help them kill the reptiles as they tried to crawl from the flames. We rolled the log over and ultimately killed four rattlesnakes, four pilot snakes, a cotton-mouthed moccasin and a chicken snake. Two others were burned beyond recognition, and one, perhaps more, escaped. At least thirteen diverse but apparently congenial hibernators had withdrawn to this mid-winter retreat. Two of the rattlesnakes and the chicken snake were all coiled up together, leading one of the bystanders to remark that "cold weather makes strange bedfellows." Later that spring of 1922, five pilot snakes and eight rattlers were killed on our place.

The water moccasins bothered us most when we tried to gig frogs at night in the slough. We would see great numbers of them swimming about in the water or lying on overhanging branches, where they would slither along and then drop *kerplunk!* into the water. We were never able to kill any of them as they darted about and slithered away, and this made us hate them all the more.

Our luck was not much better with the frogs. We worked from the boat, one rowing while the other, with a carbide light attached to his hat, used the gig. Frog legs brought about a dollar and a quarter a dozen in town, but we managed to sell only a few. This was annoying, for considering all the croaking, one would think the swamps were filled with frogs. Perhaps this was the basis for a story that was told locally. An old swamp dweller was approached by a man who dealt in bullfrog skins. The old fellow told the dealer he could supply ten thousand skins, and the dealer ordered him to ship the whole batch. Soon the dealer received a single frog skin with a note attached: "Sorry, this here is all the frog skins there was. The noise had me fooled."

One time I heard a frog squeaking quite earnestly. I found it in the process of being devoured by a snake, with only its head sticking out of the reptile's mouth. When I lunged at the snake, the frog popped out, apparently none the worse for such a harrowing experience. Another time Will and I found a frog caught in a duel between two snakes, each of which had a frog leg in its mouth, pulling in opposite directions. When we disturbed them, they loosened their holds and the frog hopped away. Evidently frog legs are a tasty dish for snakes as well as humans.

Although we were troubled with rattlesnakes and cotton-mouthed moccasins, the most tormenting and irritating of all creatures were the mosquitoes. They were, as Will Carlton aptly observed, "leeches perched on wings." Aside from the pure annoyance of their stings, the malaria which nearly everyone had at one time or another was enough to cause thoughtful folks to have much more dread of the belated, rather than the immediate, effects of those stings.

94

During our years in Arkansas I knew of only two people in our area who died from malaria, but that was twice as many as died from any single natural cause in the same period.

During the warm weather seasons of our first year or two in the backwoods, mosquitoes filled the air to such an extent that we could hear an almost constant buzzing throughout the day. They made life miserable for us as we tried to go about our business of clearing land and getting our houses built. I think the worst thing about all the timber work we did was having to contend with the mosquitoes.

According to *The British Medical Journal,* mosquitoes prefer to bite white males who are unwashed, asleep and wearing rough clothes. Most of the time, in one way or another, we pretty much fitted that description, but I noticed that the mosquitoes seemed to like us just as well when we were washed, awake, and dressed up in our Sunday best. They never turned down an opportunity.

There was some respite from them early in the mornings, but they were bad at all times. We dressed in various ways to avoid them, even experimenting, despite the heat, with long underwear. This proved no more effective than trying to wear two shirts, which they seemed to penetrate with ease. Finally, to make it as difficult as possible for them around our faces, necks, and shoulders, where they seemed to be worst, we hit upon the scheme of wearing a heavy work jacket over a thick shirt and something under the hat that would extend down over the back of the neck and as far down on the face as possible. A flour sack, slit down one side, was well suited for this purpose. And of course we wore canvas work gloves. We also tried oil of citronella, the standard mosquito repellent back then, and discovered the truth of the observation that oil of citronella will sometimes make a mosquito so ill that he is unable to bite you for two or three minutes. It was soon sweated off anyway. There just seemed to be no effective deterrent.

Later the bloodsucking little monsters got even worse. I believe it was while we were cutting timber in the fall of 1923 that they got so bad that when one of us paused for a drink of water, the other had to fan them away with his hat while the first drank. We could endure them for only three or four hours in the woods; for the rest of the day we would pick cotton, out in an open field where they were not so plentiful. One Sunday morning Mr. Keth started out to a pecan tree a few hundred feet in the woods to get a squirrel, but he couldn't make it. He solemnly related that four million mosquitoes had attacked him before he turned back (a figure he presumably arrived at by counting their legs and dividing by six). He hoped in vain for a "mosquito frost," which would kill only the insects.

And of course, as long as the nights were warm, there was no relief from them after dark; if anything, they got worse. "There is one set of mosquitoes who sting you all day," wrote Sir Charles Lyell of his visit to New Orleans in 1845, "and when they go in toward dusk, another kind comes out and bites you all night." By our time, seventy-five years later, both of these varieties had migrated to Arkansas. Dan Bennett summed it up when he wrote, "One of the hardest things to understand is how a mosquito can get along without sleep."

Even with screens we couldn't effectively keep mosquitoes out of the houses. Like all our neighbors, we had mosquito bars over the beds throughout most of the year. Often the sides of the bar were thrown up over the top during the daytime. Before going to bed at night, you shooed away any lurking ones and then dropped the sides of the bar quickly. In order to read with any degree of comfort, we often had to get in bed, under the bar, and place a kerosene lamp on a box close to the bed. Then after turning out the light to sleep, we would often hear a lone mosquito buzzing around inside. If you didn't want to spend the night chasing him and let in a lot more in the process, it was best to play a waiting game. "A mosquito," says the old saw, "is like a child. When he stops making noise, he's getting into something." By keeping a hand poised and waiting until a sting starts, you know the little demon is preoccupied, and you can get him with a quick slap.

Of course with this method you run the risk of letting a malaria carrier nibble on you, but you can't hope to stay away from the many millions of them anyway. Malaria was one occupational disease that was shared by almost everyone in the lowlands. Thad Snow put it this way: "You can't have a truly brotherly feeling for most of the human race at the moment unless you've gone blue in the face, had your teeth chatter and your bones ache with a malarial chill." I think it was malaria that afflicted the first old country boy who said he was so sick he'd have to get better to die.

So far as I know, only the female anopheles mosquito transmits malaria germs, but since we never learned to tell the girl mosquitoes from the boy mosquitoes or the anopheles from the other varieties, that information didn't help much. The first chill, followed by a fever, strikes a few days after you've been bitten by one of them. Then you get a day off, but on the third day a second and more severe attack sets in, and this pattern of every-other-day chills and fever keeps up until you either die or get well, the length and strength being determined, I suppose, by how many germs you got ahold of in the first place. Then, once you've had it, the disease has a bad habit of popping up again from time to time. There is a strain of malaria that hits you every day, but not many in our area suffered from it, to my knowledge.

Surprisingly, very little was known about the disease until a few decades ago. As late as 1898, the Surgeon-General of the U. S. Army was writing, "It has long been known that these malarial fevers result from exposure to a special kind of bad air ("malaria" is from the Latin "bad air") which is found . . . in the greatest abundance in the vicinity of marshy places. . . . Heat and moisture are essential for the development of the malarial emanations." In that respect, it would seem that knowledge of the nature of malaria had not greatly increased since the days of the Romans. Sir Charles Lyell, writing in 1849, noted "the belief of some theorists that the complaint (yellow fever) was caused by invisible animalcules, a notion agreeing singularly with that of many Romans in regard to the malaria of Italy." But even by the turn of the century, it was known that the destruction of red corpuscles was a principal evil and that the spleen was affected. In diagnosing malaria, our doctor in Marked Tree regularly examined the patient's spleen for enlargement.

Will had his first bout with malaria chills not long after we settled on the farm. He was building fences at the time and refused to quit, until I saw that he was out of his head with fever and made him go to bed. Over a four-and-a-half-year period, he suffered five or six more attacks. I ran a close second with four. The first one hit me while I was in the field working with the team. By the time I got to the house and looked in a mirror, my face was already white, the red corpuscles having been destroyed that fast. In due time the fever followed, and then my face achieved the sallow, jaundiced hue that was every malaria sufferer's mark of distinction.

We soon learned to take preventive measures against the disease. At first we tried taking one six-grain quinine capsule each night during the mosquito season. Later we learned that they could be taken just as effectively one every six hours for twenty-four hours on weekends only, thus assuring immunity for the forthcoming week.

Some people insisted they couldn't take quinine. Our doctor told us he treated such patients by saying: "Very well, I'll give you something else," whereupon he prescribed quinine camouflaged in a liquid. It was excellent psychology. They never knew the difference, he said.

Long after we left the farm, a malaria control program was instituted in that area, whereby rural houses would be sprayed with insecticides for a nominal fee of about three dollars per season.

We noticed, soon after coming to Arkansas, that one

98

way of combating the plague of mosquitoes — and thus that of malaria — was literally to get at the grass roots of the situation. Because mosquitoes like to sleep and lurk and breed in the damp hiding places offered by any growth of weeds or bushes, the yards of even the meanest-looking Negro and white cabins were kept bare of all vegetation. No grass or weeds were allowed to grow. Until I learned the reason, I was quite puzzled to see people out scraping their yards with a hoe. Then I did it too. Some people also kept small fires going at a safe distance from the house. The idea was to make as much smudge as possible, for mosquitoes don't like smoke.

My many irritating, first-hand experiences with mosquitoes ultimately inspired me to pen the following mock sonnet:

The Night Attack: A First-Hand Account

The whole night long mosquitoes buzzed around.
Did I say "long mosquitoes?" Well, that they were,
And beastly mean! In flight they made the sound
Of droning power drills in constant whir-r-r;
But here resemblance ends, for when they drilled
They made no sound at all. Like thieves they worked,
To siphon out my blood, and when, quite filled,
They left, I then could sense they gaily smirked.
For hours I fought them back, unwilling to resign
And yield them prize for all their pains —
Yet I had lost. All pains, I felt, were mine.
Aye, there's the rub! And theirs, forsooth, the gains.
    The kindest wish I'd care to make
    Is that each would die of tummy-ache.

When I become an imperial potentate, my first decree will be to abolish all mosquitoes.

The most tragic death from malaria in our neighborhood

occurred in 1921, when the little four-year-old daughter of Jim Booth died of the terrible disease. The Booths lived in a two-room shanty boat which had been pulled ashore on Dr. Baird's place adjoining ours on the north.

The little girl had a chill on Thursday, followed by a more severe one on Saturday which killed her. The father had gone to town for the week's supplies and had not yet returned when we learned of the little girl's death and went with Frank Walters, our sharecropper, up to the houseboat to help in whatever way we could. Finding Mrs. Booth and her two little boys, both older than the dead child, almost without food, we returned and brought them something to eat, as well as some coal oil for their lamp, as they had none left and it was growing dark.

Next morning Frank helped us hitch up our mules to the farm wagon and the three of us went back to the shanty boat. We put the body in the wagon, and Jim went with us, but the mother and two little boys remained behind. After we had gone about three miles through the woods, we came to a house where a fellow owned a Ford. Will persuaded him to let us use it, and we chugged and bumped on into town over a newly cut road which had not been graded or cleared of stumps.

In Marked Tree we went to an undertaker's shop where Will and I bought a pine casket for fifteen dollars (which Jim later insisted on paying back in labor). Then at a cemetery some distance from town, in the pauper's section, Will, Frank, and I dug a grave. The father sat near the body with his head buried in his hands, dressed in what was probably his only pair of "good" overalls, patched as they were, but distinguished from his "everyday" ones by their cleanness and the yet-unfaded blue of the denim. The little girl was buried without ceremony of any kind. Such were "the short and simple annals of the poor."

I was reminded of what Mark Twain said in his deep grief after the death of his beloved daughter Susy: "It is one of the mysteries of nature that a man, all unprepared, can

100

receive a thunderstroke like that and live." I did not know the little Booth girl very well, and I cannot say if she laughed and flittered about as most little girls do, or how she carried a tattered doll and played in the mud or what she looked like when she frowned or giggled, or even how she cried when, even to four-year-olds, there is too much anguish and frustration; but her parents knew, the simple father with the rough, yellow-calloused hands and the clean overalls, whose task it was to bury his baby, and the mother, whose even greater task was to see her child borne away, remaining behind to endure her woman's grief out of a patience and a privity too dark and luminous, too complex and simple, nourishing only quiet and justification and the shard of survival. "We're the people," said Ma Joad. "We go on."

The really great tragedy of the little girl's death was that it most likely could have been prevented if only Will or I had heard of her first attack. We kept quinine on hand and knew the procedure for administering it. I've often pondered why the Booths had not sought help for her. Anyone familiar with the area would simply say, "Well, that's the way people are." I understand that, I think, but still it remains a mystery to me why folks were so reckless with their lives and those of their families. I suppose it is somehow explained by ignorance and poverty and the sad fact that their existence was always a sort of marginal affair which at its best was so beset with pains and terrors that they could risk anything because they so often had to. In this respect, it was a mean way to live . . . and die.

XI MOONSHINE AND MAYHEM:

The Extra-Strength Pain Relievers

One of the principal, if temporary, ways of escaping from the aches and realities of swamp life was to drink of the cup that cheers. Officially, of course, there was nothing to put in such a cup, for the National Prohibition Act, usually called the Volstead Act, had gone into effect in January, 1920, only a few months after we bought the farm.

The law was firm, and John F. Kramer, the first Prohibition Commissioner, set out confidently to enforce it. "The law says that liquor to be used as a beverage must not be manufactured," he asserted. "We shall see that it is not manufactured. Nor sold, nor given away, nor hauled in anything on the surface of the earth or under the earth or in the air." Period. Unquote. But, as Frederick Lewis Allen observes in *Only Yesterday*, anybody who believed this "would be ready also to believe in Santa Claus, perpetual

102

motion, and pixies." I don't know if liquor ever got under the earth or in the air over our part of the country, but it was certainly made, sold, given away, and hauled all over the place.

Since booze could be manufactured or sold only for medicinal purposes, the boondocks around us were densely populated with what could only be termed "pharmaceutical concerns." The liquor business literally took to the woods, where hundreds of enterprising amateur distillers and/or quaffers supplied not only their own needs, but — at a price — those of their "drouthy neebors." The thousands of acres of woodland surrounding us made the area an ideal location for bootlegging operations. Sometimes it seemed as if there might be a still behind every tree.

Of course lots of people never had anything to do with moonshining, and a curious kind of code prevailed between "those who did" and "those who didn't." It was something like having a neighbor who beat his wife. There were two considerations: 1) maybe she needed it, and 2) although everyone might know about it, you didn't talk about it, certainly not to the wife-beater. So it was with moonshining — "judge not lest ye be judged." Some stills were run by worthless trouble-makers for their own profit, others by fairly decent men who moonshined to help feed their families when the going was rough.

The whiskey they made was usually referred to as White Mule, because of its kick. As a guess I would say that the price of White Mule averaged two to three dollars a quart. Anyone could buy it if he had a casual acquaintance with the right person — and there were plenty of "right persons" around.

Revenue agents made occasional raids, and many moonshiners armed themselves against intruders, official or otherwise. Thus it was dangerous as well as easy to stray too close to a hidden still in the woods. Parker Hood, who worked for John Haverstick as a kind of swampland cowboy, learned the hazards of rambling aimlessly over the country. I always thought Parker would have made a fine Western movie star, in the manner of Tom Mix or Ken Maynard. He was a big, handsome, well-built fellow in his early twenties, with a keen intelligence and a fine sense of humor. His main job for the Haversticks was apparently to locate their forever-straying cattle. Parker seemed to believe that lost stock would most likely be found close to homes of young ladies, and he would almost always stop to find out if his conjecture were correct. Frequently, he even waited to see if strays might show up in that vicinity. The style and breadth of Parker's amorous adventures are perhaps best shown by an incident that occurred in Marked Tree. I was walking along the street one day and saw Parker sitting between two girls in a parked car. As a greeting I called out innocently, "What are you doing for yourself, Parker?" With a wide grin he casually lifted one thumb toward the girl on his left and pointed the other thumb at the girl on his right, lapsing into a loud guffaw. I got the message.

One would have thought his greatest danger came from anxious fathers, but Parker feared more the irate moonshiners whose stills he often blundered into out in the woods. Once, while looking for stray cattle, he innocently ventured too close to a mountain-dew factory, and one of the senior executives came up shooting, wounding Parker's horse and instigating a get away that would have shamed Bob Steele or Gene Autry.

A similar incident involved Herman Davis, Arkansas' most famous hero of World War I. Davis, who came to our place on hunting trips, was a frail, tubercular fellow. In the Argonne Forest, he had captured a German machine gun nest single-handedly, killing four of its defenders. He apparently found that easier than going up against moonshiners in the woods at home. Sometime around 1922, he and several others were in our area hunting wild turkey.

104

I met some of the hunters coming out of the woods near our place, and we stood around talking for awhile as they waited for Herman to show up. When he finally appeared, he was visibly shaken, his face quite ashen and his hands almost trembling. He told us someone had shot at his dog, wounding the animal, and it had become apparent to Herman that he and the dog had wandered too close to a still. Yet he had no idea where it was, and any direction he might turn could be the wrong one. As the dog went yelping off, Herman crouched in the underbrush, well aware that going to help him might be the first step toward his own funeral. Finally things quieted down, and he was able to edge out of the woods.

When the dog turned up later, unharmed, some of us suspected that the rifle report Herman had heard was actually a dead tree limb snapping off and falling on or near the dog, frightening it. Such things had happened before.

Still, one would think that a combat veteran ought to know rifle fire when he heard it. Maybe Herman's nerves were on edge. But nobody could fault him for stepping softly in a woods full of belligerent moonshiners. Even teetotaling citizens in the area were famous for blasting away before making inquiries. A rifle slug whizzed past me one day as I was clearing brush. It turned out that the bullet had been intended for a panther that threatened to attack some young fellows camping in the woods — which was a good story, except that there were never any panthers in those parts to my knowledge. The young bucks may have been telling the truth — or they may have found an unattended still, had a sample, and spied an elusive polka dot panther.

People who knew their way around in the area usually had some idea of the general location of any stills and stayed away from those that didn't belong to them. Will and I were cutting timber on Haversticks' place one day when a fellow we knew only slightly rode up on a mule. His language was veiled, but we knew he was telling us we might run across a still. Will was diplomatic enough to let him know we wouldn't do or say anything about it if we did.

One fall, when my curiosity was running high and I seemed to have nothing better to do, I went through the woods in search of stills. Without much effort, I found the locations of five — past or present. Actually, only one of them was in operation, in a sort of no-man's-land between us and Luttrell's Landing. We suspected that it was run by Jesse Linn.

Jesse and his wife lived with another couple, the Whitten McClures, in a tiny three-room house about a mile northeast of us. Jesse and Whitten helped us with clearing work occasionally and tried to farm a sorry little piece of ground cleared out a mile or so south of Luttrell's Landing. But they had just one poor mule between them, and it was club-footed (that is, instead of walking on the soles of its fore-feet, the ankles were twisted back so that it walked on them). They even had to borrow a breaking plow — usually ours, which we were glad to lend, although I had to help Whitten carry, or as he said, "tote" it, all the way to where they lived. Their wives helped with the field work, but the acreage was just too small, and even by working some for us they could barely keep body and soul together. It was logical then to suspect that one or both of them had a still going not far away. But Whitten just wasn't the type somehow, and I always felt that Jesse ran it on his own. I remember him as a likeable, but indolent cuss whose greatest sport, upon learning that my brother and I were Masons, was to hurl at us, while we worked, a barrage of Masonic expressions which he had picked up in some unknown way.

The mash in the still I assumed to be Jesse's was open to all sorts of flies, bugs, and mosquitoes, as was the case with every other one I knew of. To me, it would have been a toss-up between drinking moonshine or slop. I think the sight of that open still would do more to reform hard drinkers than all the temperance lectures ever given.

Revenue agents had beaten me to the other four still

sites. One was on our place and two others were not far across the boundary line east. The fourth was further away, on Dr. Baird's farm. Few traces of them were left. I suspected that at least two or three of them had been operated by Lonnie Lane, a neighbor who rented our farm one year, largely, it turned out, as a blind for his bootlegging activities.

Thus my still-scouting expedition was fortunately rather uneventful. There was actually little danger, for I had had a rough idea where to look and had not gone thrashing about where I didn't belong. Even if I'd been caught at the "live" still, Jesse or whoever ran it would have known that I could be trusted not to expose it.

Since stills in operation were always in danger of being detected by the smoke they gave off, bootleggers often hedged their bets by bottling up the White Mule as it cooked off and hiding it some distance away in an unlikely spot. The discovery of such a cache was of course welcomed by anybody who imbibed, but others did not always appreciate having their land used as a moonshine drop. One such find was reported in full detail on the front page of the *Marked Tree Tribune* by its colorful editor, T. D. Harris:

> Squire Ed Pittman, teetotaler and deacon in the Baptist Church, is all wrought up about someone planting a barrel of moonshine hootch on his farm, which he unearthed Friday of last week.
>
> As the squire does not drink himself nor allow anyone working for him to do so (if he knows about it), he dumped the contents of the barrel into the St. Francis River and kept the barrel as a water container.

At that time in Arkansas, the title of squire was, I believe, held by minor judiciary officials whose duties were roughly comparable to justices of the peace. A more famous squire, Fielding's Allworthy, would have kept the whiskey

107

and dumped Ed Pittman, "teetotaler and deacon," into the river.

Despite such wrought-up defenders of morality as the good Squire Pittman, the production and consumption of liquor flourished. And of course it caused about as many pains as it relieved.

Following his periodic benders, Mr. Keth suffered some of the most ferocious hangovers I've ever witnessed. Only once that I know of did his wild sprees result in any other trouble. Just before Christmas of 1922, after four months with us out in the sticks without even sniffing a cork, he went into town and apparently tried to drink everything that sloshed. It cost him a night in jail and a fine of $14.80, which luckily enough was almost the exact sum we owed him in back wages.

Parker Hood suffered in other ways from excessive celebration. He showed up one morning after a dance sporting multiple bruises and explained that he had gotten drunk and wound up in a fight, which he'd apparently lost.

Of course liquor — either its production or consumption — was often a contributing factor in the many fights and murders that took place in our part of the country, but it certainly wasn't necessary, for sober citizens tangled as readily as drunk ones, and they found plenty of things other than stills to squabble over.

So much of the violence seemed utterly senseless — which is not to say that there's such a thing as sensible violence, but only that Arkansas Delta violence was often more absurd and meaningless than the standard varieties.

One day a young fellow, about eighteen, who lived across the river, came by our house with a dog. He told me that it belonged to one of his neighbors, whom we knew, but that he had taken it with him on his walk. When he got back home, the neighbor shot the boy and killed him. To my knowledge, nothing was ever done about it. Not long afterward in town, I saw the neighbor, a big, powerful fellow. He greeted me amiably, and we shook hands (I suppose *that's* what he intended when he put out his hand; at any rate, I shook it — lest he have something else in mind).

Some people might attribute this sort of thing to a lack of Christian influence, for there was never, during our time on the farm, a church for white people nearer than Marked Tree. But my experience leads me to doubt if church-going would have helped much. During our first fall in Arkansas, I attended a church service in a private home near Black Oak, and afterward, Herbert Odum and I were dinner guests of a family belonging to the congregation. The father later shot his son-in-law in the leg with a shotgun, and the younger man bled to death. Again, nothing was done about it. It was also my fate to encounter *this* man shortly after the killing, and I again went through the ritual of shaking hands. I never ceased to be amazed at the casual way friends and neighbors could maim and kill each other for little or no reason and afterward resume their placid, friendly manner, as though nothing had happened.

I have mentioned Parrott, the bullet-scarred man who took Will to the doctor in his boat. Not long after this errand of mercy, Parrott's old antagonist, Ben Greene, sent word that Parrott was never to pass Greene's house again, upon pain of death. Parrott ignored him and rode past — or tried to. He was stopped by a hail of bullets and died where he fell. So far as I know, no charges were filed; I doubt if the killing was ever reported to authorities, although everyone in our section knew about it. We were too far in the woods for enforcement officers to investigate every dispute or reported crime. From our location near the boundary lines of Poinsett and Crittenden counties, it was twelve or fifteen miles to either county seat. With no telephones, it took hours to reach a sheriff, and even longer for him to get there — if he could get there at all. Most county law officers wouldn't even try. It was too risky, for one thing, and they could draw their pay without working the backwoods. Besides, they had their hands full in town most of the time.

Thus "frontier justice" prevailed — people in the boon-docks literally took the law into their own hands. There wasn't much choice; it was either that or anarchy. So I sup-pose the system worked well enough to assure potential wrong-doers of swift and sudden retribution, but it also allowed such senseless goings-on as the Greene-Parrott feud.

I was doubly perplexed by Greene's killing of Parrott, for I had had some dealings with these men and found them both reasonable and considerate. Just shortly before he shot Parrott, I talked to Greene about buying some hogs. He spent considerable time with me discussing the market and telling me where I might find some porkers for sale. That same day I went to Parrott's house, and when I left, he went with me part of the way to see that I made it safely across the log spanning the upper end of Big Broadmouth. I trust that I had appreciated their thoughtfulness.

The list of similar incidents is endless. Two fellows from the country west of us spent the night with Will and me while hunting wild turkey. They seemed the best of friends, but ultimately argued over something and one killed the other. Another regular acquaintance of ours suspected his opponent in a poker game of cheating and shot him dead at the table. Even our own harmless Mr. Keth was once the victim of blind fury. Passing the attractive young wife of one of Dr. Baird's sharecroppers at a well pump one day, he spoke a few words to her, hardly more than an exchange of greetings. The girl's husband, fired by insane jealousy, ran up with a hoe and began to beat Mr. Keth with it furiously, breaking his arm and inflicting some bad bruises. Most of these crimes went unpunished; the only justice Mr. Keth got was the payment of his doctor bill, the amount of which Dr. Baird's overseer withheld from the jealous hus-band's crop share.

The eternal triangle accounted for much of the trouble. On a riverboat one day, I noticed a fellow picking with his pocket knife at a sore place on his arm. Although he was a stranger from the up-river country beyond Marked Tree, I asked him what the trouble was. He explained that a neighbor of his was living with a woman without benefit of clergy, and he said, "I figured I had as good a right to her as that feller did." Evidently "that feller" thought otherwise, and had used a shotgun to express himself. Some of the buckshot had struck my informant in the arm, and the poor disillusioned chap was performing his own surgery while putting mileage between himself and his adversary.

As with moonshining, the population seemed divided into those who quarrelled and those who didn't, and it was about as easy to do one as the other. Moreover, the lines rarely crossed. That is, if you didn't want trouble, it could be avoided easily enough; but if you hankered for a shoot-out or a knifing or just a plain old everyday two-bit country fist fight, there was always somebody ready to step up and accommodate you.

Actually, fists were seldom employed. The only fist fight I recall seeing while living in the lowlands was one in 1921 between two brothers who owned a restaurant on Main Street in Marked Tree. Whatever the trouble was, they had it out on the sidewalk in front of the cafe. Evidently the loser's connection with the firm terminated at once, for I never saw him again. Jungle rule seemed to have prevailed.

Instead of using fists to settle deep disputes, firearms were nearly always the means of deciding them, as most of the incidents I've described indicate. Some men carried revolvers as a matter of precaution at all times. I still remember how disturbed I was to see one of our young hired men take his gun out and lay it on the sill while he worked — not because he expected an Indian attack at any minute, but simply because the weapon had grown uncomfortable in his pocket.

Few of those who carried pistols were reluctant to brandish them on a moment's notice. When my brother was working as straw boss over the road crews, two Negro workers got into a dispute and one whipped out a pistol. Will instantly stepped between them and ordered the fellow to hand over his gun. He meekly surrendered it, and tragedy was averted by Will's quick action. Later, when tempers had cooled, he returned the gun, aware that the Negro might need it for self-defense any time.

Two other Negroes had a similar confrontation, one of them pulling a revolver and the other warning him with a waving forefinger, "Don't you shoot that thing! Don't you dare shoot!" But he did, twice. One was a clean miss, and the other hit the admonishing forefinger.

One year when our farm was rented to Dr. Baird, his overseer, Siah Morris, lived with me in one of our houses on Broadmouth. Mr. Morris came in from the field one day and took out two revolvers, keeping one and handing the other to me. He explained that he'd had an argument with one of the Negro sharecroppers, who had pulled a gun on him. Since he had been unarmed, he'd walked away, but he expected more trouble and wanted to prepare for it. The sharecropper and a couple of friends approached our house that evening, headed home, but to my great relief they kept on going. Tempers cooled as readily as they flared.

It is an interesting paradox that in such a violent land, there was so little thievery. Like most people in the region, we never locked our doors, whether we were at home or gone miles away, and to my knowledge, the only things ever stolen from us were a pair of pliers and some harness that stuck to a sharecropper's fingers when he moved away. (The situation was somewhat different in town, where businesses were plagued with every imaginable kind of break-in, robbery, hi-jacking, and embezzlement.)

Our experience in leaving doors unlocked somewhat paralleled that of Thoreau. In *Walden* he observed that during his life in the woods he used no lock or bolt — didn't even have them — and added that his house "was more respected than if it had been surrounded by a file of soldiers."

112

Perhaps that's a little idealistic for Arkansas. I think that in our country respect played a less important role than fear. Any potential thief knew what would happen to him if he were caught.

Some things were stolen from a neighbor on the Cummins farm up above us. Soon he rode by our house with several other men, all heavily armed. The suspect, before disappearing, had told someone that he was going to do some work for the Swank brothers. We never saw the fellow, but it certainly wouldn't have been healthy for him if that posse had found him.

Some attempts at playing policeman would have been comical if they weren't so dangerous. An elderly bachelor named Frank Hammond lived in a tent not far from us. Shaky Frank, as he was known on account of his palsy, came to our house one day when I was alone and said someone had taken things from his tent. He was armed to the teeth and hot on the trail; he'd heard a dog barking while the crime was in progress and vowed he could identify the culprit by the way his dog barked. He wanted me to take him across Big Broadmouth in our boat, for he was positive the thief was headed west, toward Haversticks'.

At the time, I was trying to get a wagon load of bundled shingles into the barn loft, and it was a hard job for one man. I would heave a few bundles into the loft, then have to go up and move them back, then down and up again. I told Shaky Frank that I would ferry him across the slough if he would first help me unload the shingles.

He laid down his shotgun and got in the wagon, while I crawled into the loft to take the bundles as he handed them to me. From above him I could see that he had a pistol in each hip pocket and a bottle of whiskey under his shirt. That didn't exactly make me the calmest shingle-shuffler in the country, but we managed to get the bundles unloaded without mishap, and I quickly deposited Shaky Frank on the opposite bank of Broadmouth and put about toward home, somewhat relieved to have the slough channel between us. I learned later that he got no further than the Haversticks', where the only serious damage was that which he and Uncle Jim Haverstick inflicted upon the whiskey bottle. Indeed, I believe they killed it. The thief — if there was one — was soon forgotten.

I don't mean to leave the impression that Shaky Frank was a harmless old lush. He was a veteran of several gunfights and was rumored to have killed at least one man. He later moved to a community known as Dub, near Marked Tree, and so terrorized a family there that one of them, a boy about sixteen, killed him with a shotgun.

Thus things were rarely dull, although it was the sort of excitement I could have done without. Writing home early in 1923, I summarized local happenings: "In fires at Marked Tree a Negro restaurant and boarding house burned, a carload of cotton was destroyed, and a cotton gin, together with $40,000 worth of cotton, went up in smoke; a Negro above Marked Tree killed two white men and escaped; and four moonshine stills near us were destroyed by revenue officers."

Looking over later reports, one concludes that things got worse instead of better. In 1924 and 1925, the *Marked Tree Tribune* carried stories relating to almost every crime and act of violence known to man, including arson, incest, embezzlement, and white slavery, as well as the more popular pastimes of robbery, murder, and making moonshine. Admittedly, some of these escapades involved former citizens whose exploits elsewhere were such that news of them spread back to Marked Tree like the backwash from a garbage scow. Take for instance the case of Ira Smith, who went off to Hornersville, Missouri, and got himself killed one fine autumn Sunday in 1925. Reporting the event, the *Marked Tree Tribune* reminded readers that Smith had "cut some bad capers in Marked Tree" earlier that year. Apparently he had "threatened to 'mop up' with the entire police force of the town and it required three or four men to finally land him in jail." After a few days in the pokey, Smith was released "upon promise to leave never to return."

114

Noting his violent demise in Missouri, the editor laconically observed, "He kept his word."

Even more spectacular were the adventures of Cowboy Jack Globo, a sort of resident bad guy who, in the space of only a few months was involved in three shootings and countless brawls before a deputy finally killed him in a gunfight at Lepanto, twelve miles from Marked Tree, in March, 1925.

In February of that year, a headline in the *Tribune* proclaimed "Robberies & Holdups Galore Since 1925 Began." Said the editor, "Something must be done to stop this kind of business, or Marked Tree will soon regain the name it had 20 years ago" (suggesting that life had never been quite idyllic there).

In the first ten months of 1926, there were twelve murders in the area, most of them down in our part of the woods, which shortly became known as "No-Man's-Land," a title as lacking in distinction as it was in originality. There was a similar badland up in the Missouri bootheel, just across the state line. There, one of the old-timers, commenting on the high number of murders, said, "It is not to our discredit — as anyone can see, we have so many more people that need killing." I suppose the same could have been said for our part of the country.

Perhaps it is significant to note that almost all of the encounters I have listed were between whites. Although Negroes similarly fought among themselves, I doubt if they inflicted as much damage to each other; and I recall not more than three instances of trouble between blacks and whites. At any rate, it is a sobering fact that during the time we lived there, acts of violence were the occasion of more adult deaths in the area than all other causes put together.

XII THE PASSING PARADE:

Fun and Games

If you didn't drink or fight, life in the Arkansas lowlands forty years ago offered little in the way of diversion. However, for the first few years after we settled there, I got all the entertainment I needed just by observing the strange things that took place in the social lives of local inhabitants.

I've mentioned going to a church service the first fall I was on the farm. This had been at the invitation of the Odums, with whom Will and I had stayed while building our house. Back in Ohio, those who didn't have cars went to church in buggies — but a buggy would have been as out of place in Arkansas as Mr. Keth at a temperance meeting. I don't believe I ever saw one in our neighborhood. The Odums, with Etta and Herbert and a neighbor boy, came by the house that Sunday morning in the farm wagon, and we made extra seats by putting a couple of 2 x 6's across the wagon sideboards. (I later learned that this was quite common; Wayman Hogue in *Back Yonder,* writing about the Ozarks, mentions "a board stretched across the wagon bed for seats.")

We bumped along three or four miles, over roads that had been rutted and slashed up by wagons used in hauling logs through the woods, before finally reaching the home where services were to be held. There was no Sunday School or other ceremony; the "services" consisted entirely of a fiery sermon delivered by the preacher, a lay minister who took off from his farm work to hold church every third Sunday. He was hardly a spell-binding orator, but there was no doubting his sincerity.

The congregation gathered in one room of the house for the sermon, some sitting on the bed, some on a log plank, others on store boxes or a trunk or the two or three chairs.

After the service, Herbert Odum and I went to dinner at the home of some people he knew. I was intrigued to learn that they had a record player, which even in 1919 was still something of a novelty, particularly in the backwoods. I saw only one other "talking machine" while we were on the farm. It belonged to a tent-dweller across the river from us, who told me he would never have bought such a thing had he not been drunk. He had apparently acquired the record player while on a spree in Memphis. Radio was of course unknown in our area.

After we ate, a boy in the family, about Herbert's age, took out some records and began to play them for us. Suddenly, in the midst of one selection, the boy decided he didn't like the music. Instead of shutting off the machine in a normal way, he shouted a loud oath and kicked it furiously until the lever flipped to "Off" with an audible snap. Satisfied, the boy resumed his role as genial host.

While we were listening to the records, a neighbor woman called on the lady of the house, who read to her visitor from the Bible. As she read, snuff juice dripped from her mouth. (It was her husband who later killed their son-in-law, a story I related earlier.)

117

I soon grew accustomed to such goings-on, but it was almost too much for me that day, having just arrived from our considerably more sedate and "civilized" surroundings in Ohio, where ladies did not dip snuff and people usually tried to refrain from kicking the furniture in the presence of guests.

The subject of snuff deserves a little more attention here. Perhaps no other social habit of the frontier survived so late and died so fast as the lively art of snuff-dipping. It may be a wild, foolish guess, but I doubt if there are ten people under fifty in the U.S. today who still dip snuff. In our time back in Arkansas, however, the big majority of the country people — both men and women — were snuff-dippers. Garrett's Snuff was known in every household. There were other brands, of course, but Garrett's was the old stand-by. As I recall, it came in glass jars, (always utilized as beverage glasses when empty), tins, and small sacks. It was cheaper than any other form of tobacco, and this no doubt accounted for its popularity. Next in preference were chewing tobacco and pipes — the cost of cigars was prohibitive, and cigarettes had not yet come into common use, except as "roll-your-owns." Incidentally, I never saw a woman in our region with a cigarette during the first six years of the 1920's. It was not until 1928 that I first saw a cigarette advertisement which associated the female sex with cigarette smoking — and how veiled its message was!

There were several ways of using snuff. Most dippers put it between the upper or lower gums and the lip, usually in front but sometimes farther back; some even chewed it a little. Women often employed what was known as a "toothbrush," a willow twig frayed on one end, dipped in snuff and pushed back into the jaw to chew on throughout the day.

Testifying to the massive local consumption of snuff was a "snuff tree" about four miles from us on the Black Oak Road. This was a large dogwood, more dead than alive, entirely covered with dozens and dozens of snuff containers

118

of every size and description. It would have been a fitting subject for Ripley.

I got a second lesson in frontier etiquette at the only party I can remember attending in Arkansas. This was a dance at John Haverstick's house in the winter of 1923. I believe there were only a dozen or so guests, and it was anything but formal. The ladies arrived in knee boots, then changed to shoes for the party, but we men wore our hip boots throughout, even dancing in them. Amusements were largely limited to dancing, eating popcorn, and playing Pitch, a popular country card game. There was no liquor or trouble, but nobody "played the soft pedal," and a genuine rip-roaring time was had by all.

However, some of our neighbors' social habits disturbed me a bit at first. Conventional "store-bought" refreshments were in short supply at the party, and I watched in horrified fascination as one young miss peeled a stick of gum, wadded it into her mouth, chewed a few minutes, and then handed it to a second, who joyfully repeated the process and then casually gave the soggy wad to a third girl who popped it into her mouth with equal aplomb. Apparently such habits were "come by honest," as the country folk say: during the course of the same evening, the third girl's mother, a pleasant widow named Della Clymer, was approached by a salty old widower who'd expended his supply of snuff, and Della promptly provided him with a "dip" from her own tin.

Four of us spent most of the evening playing Pitch. In fact, we became so engrossed in the game that we lost track of time, until someone noticed it was five A.M.! Perhaps the long, lonely days and weeks in the wilderness had whetted our appetites for companionship and recreation more than we knew. Will and I decided it was too late (or too early!) for us to bother going to bed. Weary, but somehow rejuvenated, we trudged happily home as the first light of wintery dawn spread above Big Broadmouth.

That, as I recall, was our only organized social affair in Arkansas. We once went to a Negro dance, but our presence there was more in the nature of interested bystanders rather than active participants in a party. The affair took place in the spring of 1922 at a small cabin a mile or so up the St. Francis from Big Broadmouth. Will and I had spent almost three years in the sticks with hardly any "night life" to speak of — there was just too much day life — and when we learned by the grapevine of the coming event, we looked forward to it with more than a little enthusiasm. Unfortunately, we made a practice of leaving our good clothes at a friend's house in Marked Tree (since that was the only place we had had occasion to wear them), but we decided that our cleanest and best work clothes would suffice for a backwoods get-together. However, we had invited Lee, Tom, and Dick Grafton — the single fellows among our renters — to go with us, and we failed to reckon with the splendor of their sartorial equipage. They joined us dressed in Sunday best, hard collars and all.

The five of us walked through the woods to the Leatherwood place, where we crossed Big Broadmouth in little boats, then walked on up along the river. The dance was well under way when we arrived. Seeing the mass of dark faces bobbing and swinging on every side in the feeble flickers of coal-oil lamps that faintly lighted the scene, I could understand what Milton meant about "darkness visible." Music was provided by a fiddle and encouragement by an animated caller, who chanted and shouted and cajoled the dancers as they swung each other around and around. At intervals the crowd cleared back and stood talking and yelling while the more talented performed singly or in couples, spinning and shaking in a seemingly spontaneous manner, inspired by the fiddling. The festivities were still in high gear when, after a few hours, we left, having drunk deeply, if briefly, of life and laughter and music in a time and place when radio or television were yet unknown.

Another source of amusement and intrigue was the speech habits of our Arkansas neighbors. My ears soon became attuned to the slow drawl, the long r's, and the

120

dropped g's, even broad vowels in the strangest places ("drank" for "drink"; "tard" for "tired") and "yawl," a corruption of the more gracious Deep South "you-all." But it was a long time before I grew accustomed to people "carrying" each other to town or "wholping" their children. Also strange to me was the practice of applying "Mister" to one's Christian name rather than the surname — to most of our neighbors I quickly became "Mr. Roy," rather than "Mr. Swank" or just plain Roy. Although this usage was practiced by nearly everyone at some time or another, it was more commonly applied to those in a higher social station. I recall hearing a poor grandmother teaching her little grandchildren always to use "Mr." or "Mrs." with the first name of their landowner or his wife. Prefixing "Mr." to one's Christian name was also an almost invariable practice of Negroes in addressing white people. The same appellation of respect is frequently applied to deity, too, as when a Negro once commented, after we'd killed a rattlesnake, "I wonder who make snakes. I know Mr. Lord didn't do it."

At one time I was doing some work for John Haverstick. Working with me was one of John's Negro sharecroppers — a self-styled preacher — who would leave off the "Mr." in speaking to me. I didn't want to be an exception to the rule, and I didn't like the fellow anyway, so after a few times, I said, "Didn't you leave off something?" After that he left off my name altogether.

Many of our neighbors thought that Will and I looked much alike. We were walking down Main Street in town one day when we met a Negro acquaintance of Will's. He first looked puzzled, then his face lit up, and he exclaimed, "Why, I like to of not knowed you-all apart." An interesting switch on the old saw that all Negroes look alike.

The speech of both Negroes and whites was larded with interesting malapropisms, such as "vericle veins," "cute innerjession" (acute indigestion), "perfection (infection) set in," "block-and-tickle" (for block-and-tackle pulley), "petition" for "partition," and "spontaneous" for "simultaneous."

121

We laughed at Mr. Keth, whose English was better than most, when he told of getting lost in the woods and going in circles, wandering repeatedly upon the same log pile. "I came three *successful* times to that same pile of logs," he said.

I first discovered "carry" for "take" when Herbert Odum said he was going to "carry" his girl to Tyronza. Since Tyronza was twelve miles away and he wasn't very big, this sounded like quite an undertaking. Where we were accustomed to use "carry," they said "tote" — as in "Tote that log."

Another local idiom that gave me trouble was the use of "evening" for what we had always considered "afternoon." The first instance of this was when I had some work to do and asked Herbert to help me next morning. He declined but agreed to do it "tomorrow evenin'," meaning of course an hour or two after the noon meal. Assuming he considered "evening" to be "almost sundown," as I did, I told him to forget it, for I knew we couldn't finish the job at night.

As I've mentioned, "whelp" or "wholp" was used for "whip." Fathers threatened their sons: "How'd you like to get wholped?"

If a person wanted you to test the weight of something, he would say "Feel the heft of this." "Spelling" meant relieving; someone might offer to take your place in swinging a sledge by saying, "Here, let me spell you a bit." In reading the *Journal* of Lorenzo Dow, I was interested to find a similar usage in his account of a trip to Virginia in the early 1800's: "In company with Brother Mead I was on foot when a young gentleman . . . on his way home, dismounted and constrained me to ride; thus we three *spelled* each other alternately" (italics mine). Dow was a New Englander, but his speech was influenced by wide travels in the South.

What we know as porches in Ohio were called stoops by Arkansans. Apparently there is as much historical basis for the Southern as for the Northern terms. According to W. E. Woodward, in *The Way Our People Lived,* "The early

English Colonials knew nothing of porches, and only learned of them from the early Dutch settlers of New York." "Stoop" of course comes from the Dutch "stoep." Like Mr. Keth, our Pennsylvania Dutchman, the word had somehow filtered into the Southland.

I was always something of a bookworm, as was Will, but out in the wilderness our choice of reading material was largely limited to pulp magazines and occasional newspapers. There was nothing resembling rural mail delivery, but the girls at the post office in town saved back issues of the *Marked Tree Tribune* for us. It mattered little that the news was sometimes a month old. If anything big happened, we usually heard about it in a day or two from someone passing on the river or from a neighbor who'd been into town. If it wasn't big enough for that, it was too insignificant to get "het up over."

I read the *Tribune* mostly for the wondrous flavor of the editor's reporting style. It would be best described as lush neo-Victorian, uniquely blended with country idiom and liberally laced with old-fashioned journalese, galloping hyperbole, and a flair for the melodramatic. The *Tribune* never allowed people merely to die or even pass away; they were always "visited by the death angel." Peace officers were "minions of the law," Negroes were "darkies," residents of Marked Tree were "denizens" (usually "of the best little town on the face of His sweet earth"), and people who wrote anonymous letters criticizing the best little town or its denizens were "cowardly whelps." When rashes of law-breaking and violence erupted, the editor always issued the same jeremiad: "Whither are we drifting?"

The report of sixteen-year-old Noreen Bullard's sudden death drew upon the writer's deepest talents. Noreen, whose "bright spirit and cheerful demeanor made her the object of great affection and many friendships," had been working as a salesgirl in a local store when she suddenly grew ill and went home, telling her employer she would return the next day if she felt better. "But alas," continued the *Tribune's*

123

story, "Noreen never came back, for she had contracted ptomaine poison in something she had eaten or drunk, and the death angel visited. Her young soul was wafted back to its Maker, there to repose in Eternity." Next week, readers learned that the "ptomaine poison" had apparently been brought about by "some fatal liquid" intended to induce an abortion and given the girl by E. P. Burton, "prominent citizen, banker, and planter," who, it was reported by a writer with a surplus of prepositions, was "under the alleged charge of murder in connection with the death of Noreen Bullard of this city."

Even with such sensational news, the editor had trouble winning new subscribers and frequently extolled the virtues of the local paper in front-page editorials that ran the full range of emotions. Here is one of the more waggish ones:

> Have you heard about the fellow who wasn't taking his home paper? Well, sir, they say he sold his cotton four cents a pound below the market price; then his property was sold for taxes because he didn't read the sheriff's warning notice; he lost $10 betting on Mollie McCarthy ten days after another horse won the race; he was arrested and fined for hunting out of season, just because he didn't know when the season was; his wife ran off and left him because she couldn't tell when the stores were having their bargain sales; and his best friend had been buried three months before he heard he was dead."

If any new subscribers signed up, they must have done so on credit, for this sad tale appeared later:

> It is reported that one of the fastidious newly-married ladies of this town kneads bread with her gloves on. This incident may be somewhat peculiar, but there are others. The editor of this paper needs bread with

his shoes on; he needs bread with his shirt on; he needs bread with his pants on, and unless some of the delinquent subscribers to this "Old Ray of Freedom" pony up before long, he will need bread without anything on, and Arkansas is no Garden of Eden in the winter time.

Apparently that got some results. One reader was so moved as to send in a cash renewal, enclosing a scriptural admonition: "Go thy way, eat thy bread with joy, and drink thy wine with a merry heart." "It's a wise man," replied the editor, "who knows his fellow's merit."

The Tribune columns written by community correspondents or "stringers" filled (unintentionally, of course) the role now played in most papers by comic strips. These were amateurish but enthusiastic reports of happenings in out-of-the-way places like Black Oak, Tyronza, Cherry Bean, Dub, and Pilgrim Rest. A story from the Nichols School News is typical:

> Church services were held here last Saturday night, Sunday and Sunday night by Elder Frank Cook. His subject on Sunday and Sunday night was "Exposure of Holy Rollerism." He didn't make it quite plain what a Holy Roller is. He did not hardly know himself. He just simply bit off more than he could chew. This Saturday night, Sunday and Sunday night, there will be services held here by one of God's ministers — by a real Christian, who does not belittle other churches and their beliefs.

But nobody could outdo the superintendent of Negro schools, who conducted a column filled with reports of such phenomena as Dr. J. W. Gates, "the fiery pulpiteer of Arkansas," who once "touched the bell chord of glory and turned over the canteen of love in our hearts." Another

125

preacher, described as "the pulpit wizard," successfully "let down the lead line of prayer and pulled on the bell chord of faith, in that he touched the crystal gushing springs of that life-giving stream which set our souls on fire and the oil of gladness down did stream." Perhaps the typesetter was overcome by it all, for a few lines down in the same report was the news that "Mrs. Cora Bethany isucmfury and was buried Jan. 17." If the galloping prose didn't get you, "isucmfury" surely would.

I suspect that for a lot of white people, the Negroes themselves provided one source of entertainment. The colored people said and did funny things and they ate watermelon and had lots of rhythm, and if life got dull for the local white toughs, they could always find a Negro to scare. This was mostly harmless, of course, in the way that tying cans to dogs' tails, throwing kittens in the creek, and putting turtles on their backs are harmless.

What little I learned about Negroes came mostly from what I was told about them, plus a few random personal contacts. Although we tried on various occasions to get Negro sharecroppers, we were never successful in finding any who were interested.

Once I made two trips to see a Negro in Marked Tree about working for us. Each time I was met at the door by a colored woman who, when I asked for her husband by name, told me, "Nawsaah, I don't reckon I knows him." The fellow who'd recommended the Negro insisted that he lived there, so I made a third try. This time I told the woman what I wanted — which I should have done at first — whereupon she then called the man to the door. When I told him we were looking for a sharecropper, he said, "Yessah, I'll be down next Tuesday." But for some reason "next Tuesday" never came. Another Negro across the river also agreed to come on a certain day, yet never showed up. After that we became skeptical of such promises and gave up trying to hire Negroes.

Some of them possessed an interesting point of view. A

Negro renter once made a loan of five hundred dollars to a worthless, untrustworthy colored doctor. A white man told the lender that he would never see his money again.

"Nawsah, it all right," the colored fellow replied. "You see, I works him. When I'se sick, I has him come, and then lets the pay go on the note — and sometimes I has him come when I *ain't really* sick."

I passed a Negro house in town one day, and heard two ladies on the porch philosophizing. One of them mentioned how exhausted she was, and the other asserted, "The Lawd say the *lilies* don't work," suggesting from her tone that she was invoking scripture to explain her own distaste for labor. The subject turned to domestic violence, and one of the women sighed, "A pusson sho' do get tard of fightin'." I assumed it was the voice of experience. I was reminded of the time I was in a store in Marked Tree when wild screams erupted from across the street. A Negro woman appeared, running for dear life and letting out a yell at every jump. I was puzzled that no one seemed to be chasing her, but the storekeeper, who knew her domestic habits better than I did, calmly explained that it was a common occurrence. "Her husband was probably mad and picked up a knife, then she got scared and ran. She'll go back home after awhile." Later I learned that this was exactly what happened.

Our nearest Negro neighbors were a man and his wife living alone and off to themselves in a small clearing about a mile from us. One morning we heard someone calling us from outside the house. It was the colored lady, standing in the front yard, according to custom, rather than coming on the porch and knocking on the door. She told us her husband was having terrible stomach pains and asked if I could come to see about him. I went with her, gave the man some milk of magnesia from our supplies, and he soon recovered. They thanked me profusely and were so impressed by the healing powers of the medicine that they took the name of it from me and later bought a supply in town. I was rather intrigued by the furnishings in their home. They had straw matting on the floor of one room, and with perhaps one exception that was the only time I ever saw floor covering in any house in that area. Gumbo and carpeting mixed only too well.

For a time our folks sent us a subscription to a newspaper back in Ohio — the *Columbus Dispatch*. Ironically enough, we sometimes got as much big news about our part of Arkansas from it as we did from the *Marked Tree Tribune*. It was in the *Dispatch*, for instance, that we first read about the sale of bonds for a mammoth drainage project in Poinsett County, in which Marked Tree is located. The project was claimed to be part of the largest drainage construction program in the world, involving a massive primary ditch twenty-two feet deep and extending from the Missouri bootheel southward across Arkansas to the St. Francis River. Plans originally called for the ditch to empty into the St. Francis a few miles below where we lived, and bonds totaling $400,000 were sold for that purpose. However, it seems that the contractors acted independently of bond issues and increased their "take" by shortening the ditch so that it emptied a few miles above our property. Apparently the cost to the taxpayers was the same as if the ditch had continued the entire distance provided by the sale of bonds. No taxes, however, were assessed on our land, as would have been the case if the ditch had extended to its original juncture with the St. Francis.

The ditch was not completed until late in 1923, construction being hampered to a certain extent, I believe, by the efforts of several irate farmers living below us to dynamite the levee in an attempt to divert the water into its natural drainage channel extending several miles to the south. However, none of these plots succeeded. Apparently the saboteurs had only dynamite that was old and ineffective.

We were probably not so adversely affected as those south of us; at any rate, we did not try to blow up anything, even though the drainage ditch contributed to local flood conditions in years of heavy rainfall.

128

During the rainy season of 1922, flood waters had risen two or three feet higher than ever before, except during an overflow, which occurs only when the Mississippi levee breaks. Heavy downpours in 1923 raised the level even higher than the year previous. Weather records kept by a lumber company in Marked Tree showed that rainfall for the first five months of 1923 was nearly thirty-six inches, or almost as much as the average annual rainfall back in Ohio. "This is the rainiest goldarn spring I've ever seen, and I reckon I've seen a thousand," said an old-timer earnestly. Finally, things got so bad that officials agreed to dynamite the drainage levee, thus letting much of the water go the way it would have gone naturally, reaching the river farther south.

But for most folks in our area, floods were a regular occurrence, and I think people looked forward to high waters. I know I did. It was a time for leisure, a time when you could rest or read or go boating around to call on neighbors, or maybe just sit down and meditate without being troubled that there was cotton to plow or timber to cut (maybe there was, but you couldn't do much about it in hip boots or a johnboat). Then, too, there was the knowledge that on the flooded lands the sediment would make a rich soil even richer.

Everyone did not fare so well, however. The flood waters of 1923 caused a great deal of anguish to many poor sharecroppers whose homes were in low places. Among them was a widower named Payne and his daughter Georgia, who was about fifteen or sixteen years old when they first settled on Dr. Baird's place in 1922.

Mr. Payne was a feisty Englishman from near Bristol. He still spoke with faint traces of cockney, using the long "i" in "either" and "neither" — pronouncing them "eye-ther" and "nye-ther." It particularly amused us to hear him searching for his pipe, which he was always misplacing. "Me poipe, me poipe; I can't find me poipe," he would repeat over and over as he searched around frantically for it.

Georgia was an attractive, sensible girl whose fate it was to be stuck, as it were, out in the wilderness with few companions her own age, no opportunity for schooling, and little to look forward to except keeping house for her father and working in the fields during the hoeing and harvest seasons. I don't believe she got to town once during the two years they were on Dr. Baird's farm.

One of Georgia's few pleasures came from cheap magazines, with their advertisements offering opulent premiums for selling a certain amount of shoddy merchandise — sachet, perfume, cheap jewelry, good luck charms, magic rings, or whatever. Whenever she came by with such trivia, we always tried to help her out by buying something.

One day when the flood waters were rising, I rowed up Big Broadmouth to the Payne's house. On the way up I saw a rabbit dart into a hollow log which had fallen into the slough. Georgia went back to the tree with me and sat in the boat at one end of the log while I went to the other end and poked with a stick. When the rabbit popped out at her end, she trapped it like an expert. I killed it, peeled off the hide, and presented it to the Paynes for supper that night.

Sometime later, the rising water drove Payne's chickens out of their coops in a low area. They took refuge under the house, which like all others in the area, was set up off the ground on blocks. I helped Georgia and her father recover the stupid birds, crawling under the house to grab a few, then handing them up to the girl or her father, who took them into the house where they had placed boxes to be used as roosts. We managed to save a hundred and seventeen, losing only three in the process.

Finally the flood waters got up in all the houses on Dr. Baird's place, even the Payne's, which was built on the highest spot of ground. Their house, unlike the others, had only one story, so they moved into the upstairs of an adjoining tenant house, sticking a stovepipe out of an upper window to accommodate their cookstove. When the flood

130

subsided, they moved back, but soon another surge of rising water sent them upstairs a second time. Again the water went down, and again the floods came. This was too much for Georgia and her father. They gathered their few possessions together, hired a boat, and moved away for good.

Another of Dr. Baird's sharecroppers had a unique experience during that year of heavy downpours. He was visiting a young married couple in the neighborhood one evening when rain began to fall in thick sheets. The storm raged on without letup, until finally, toward midnight, the husband, indicating the only bed in the house, said, "Well, I reckon we'll all have to sleep like a brood of pigs in one bed." And, with the husband tactfully in the middle, they did.

Dr. Baird somehow attracted renters and sharecroppers with their own distinctive flavor. In addition to the Paynes, there were the Rodins — all eighteen of them, including Mama, Papa, and sixteen stair-stepped little Rodins. Two other families indicated the prevalence of early marriages in that part of the country; one new matron was only twelve when married, another thirteen. "Get 'em young, treat 'em rough, and tell 'em nothin' " was the prevailing male attitude toward matrimony.

The Moon brothers rounded out our complement of unusual neighbors. One of them was the father of several children, the youngest, like Wallstreet Panic Snopes, still without a name at three years of age. The father quipped that he was too poor to give him a name. He made a fine corn crop one year, however, so the lad may have gained an identity.

The Moon brothers came down to our place one Sunday when Will and I were in the field. We normally didn't work on Sundays, but it was threatening rain, and we were anxious to get in some shocks of slip-jerked corn. Will saw the Moons approaching and, invoking his dry sense of humor, whispered to me to let on that we thought it was Saturday. As we talked, one of the Moon boys remarked about us working on the Sabbath. I laughed and told him that this was Saturday, that he was a day ahead. He let out a loud guffaw, slapped his leg, and looked at his brother as if we were crazy. I suppose we, in our own way, were as strange to them as they were to us.

The heavy rains continued all through 1923. By late December, 77.97 inches had fallen, with measurable precipitation on a hundred and twenty-five days. That was almost six and a half feet of water for the year, and more fell before the first of January, 1924.

"Looks like it'll rain for forty days and nights straight," said one old-timer during a downpour, "and then drizzle till it quits." During a short break in the high waters, an elderly Negro woman was moved to observe, "Seems we have some kind of a drought about every year. If we don't have a dry drought, we have a wet one." Our swamp droughts were usually wet ones.

XIII FIRES OF TRIBULATION:

The Rains Came, the Earth Trembled, and the Flames Raged

After our Mississippi renters left in the fall of 1922, we made several attempts to find Negro sharecroppers, but for one reason or another were unsuccessful. Apparently many of them were flocking northward into the Missouri bootheel, where the boll weevil had not yet penetrated.

Finally, in the early spring of 1923, we acquired a white 'cropper named Billy Warthin (whom we always knew as "Uncle" Billy, according to the local custom of addressing middle-aged men by that title).

By that time Will and I had moved back into our original home on Big Broadmouth. Uncle Billy and his wife lived in the other house nearby, separated from us only by the barn, where he stabled his livestock — a horse, six hogs, two cows, a calf, and a flock of chickens. I never knew of another sharecropper so affluent.

Uncle Billy really tried to get ahead in the world (although we later heard that his efforts in this direction included some light-fingered forays among his neighbors' goods). He even furnished himself — that is, he bought his own groceries and other supplies, rather than taking advances from us.

Mrs. Warthin was a thin, gaunt woman, in the lean pattern of most backwoods people. The Warthins were childless and never seemed to have any company or go anywhere, except for Uncle Billy's periodic trips to town for supplies. She rarely left the place, and I often reflected on what a drab, deadening existence it must have been for her, although I doubt if life with Uncle Billy was entirely uneventful. His most distinguished characteristics were his red hair and fiery temper. Soon after moving onto our place, he took pneumonia, and for two weeks his intake of solid food consisted entirely of half a biscuit. However, his temper thrived. One day when he was hardly able to sit up, his wife came to our house, crying. She said he got mad and had just thrown a poker at her. "If it had hit me, it would of killed me," she sobbed.

There was a rash of house fires that spring, foreshadowing our own coming disaster. Shortly after Uncle Billy's recovery, the roof of their house caught fire, apparently from an overheated chimney or from sparks that had dropped near it. Luckily, Uncle Billy, Will, and I were not far away. We raced to the house, climbed a ladder that was conveniently leaning against it, and smothered the flames, but not before a large patch of shingles near the flue had burned.

The Haversticks were less fortunate. Somehow a fire got started in a few dead trees standing in new ground which had been under crop only a year or two. The wind began to carry sparks from one dead trunk to another and finally to a tenant house at least two hundred feet from the nearest tree. I had watched some of the trees catch fire, but had no idea a live spark could fly so far as to reach the house. However, there were some sacks of inflammable mule feed on

134

the porch, and 35,000 shingles had been stored inside just a week earlier. The whole building was flaming furiously in a few seconds. There was nothing to fight it with, but I doubt if even the best fire department in the country could have saved anything.

Later that spring we found two more sharecroppers, Fred Case and Reber Kennedy. They moved their families into our houses down on the south line, and for the first time since they were built, all four houses were occupied.

It was just our luck that, with everything beginning to shape up, 1923 turned out to be one of the worst cotton years of the decade. Planting was delayed by the heavy spring rains, a bad condition made worse, as I've described, by the floodwaters brought down through the drainage ditch and dumped into the St. Francis just above us. Then we had an exceptionally late frost — May 10 — and much of the young cotton was damaged. As a result of all these unfortunate circumstances, Uncle Billy's crop produced less than two full bales. Will and I harvested exactly two bales, which faithful Mr. Keth helped pick, averaging seventy-three pounds a day at $1.00 a hundred and board. The Cases and the Kennedys fared even worse. They left early that fall, and Uncle Billy moved away in November, adding to his meager store a horse collar, bridle, and a few other things belonging to us.

Early in September of that year, Mother, Dad, our brother Clarence, and sisters Gertrude and Florence came from Ohio to visit us. They got as far as Marked Tree in their Ford. We met them there and brought them out to the farm in our trusty wagon, pulled by Sam and Rhody. We were of course thrilled to see all of them. Mother and Dad had helped us get started financially, spiritually, and otherwise — and we felt we owed them a great deal. What was their reaction to our new land? Perhaps it is sufficient to say that they were not overly enthusiastic about the location, lack of roads, mosquitoes, snakes, and stumps. They stayed only a few days.

A month or so later, I was alone in the house one day when a loud rumbling began to roll across from the south, as if a massive freight train were roaring up the slough. When the house began to rattle, I ran outside but had hardly hit the ground when all the commotion stopped. After taking a look to make sure there were no trains in the slough or perhaps a dinosaur in the backyard, I began to suspect that the disturbance had been caused by an earthquake, for we had been told that such tremors were common, although we had never experienced any. My theory was borne out by the discovery of a number of cracks or fissures in the gumbo, an inch or two wide, running parallel to Big Broadmouth.

Will had been in town at the time, and later, in a letter home, reported the events of the day with his ex-newspaperman's keen eye for detail:

> The first and more serious shock came about 10:30 Sunday morning, November 11, lasting for perhaps half a minute. I was in the Arkansaw Drug Store in Marked Tree at the time and being in a brick building, the shocks were of course somewhat exaggerated by the jarring of the building. Articles fell clattering from the shelves, and the building rocked with a wave-like motion, while a heavy rumbling noise, somewhat like continuous distant thunder, seemed to come from the south and pass northward. In a three-story brick building nearby several cracks were made in the walls. In the First National Bank a plate glass window was broken — a previous bullet hole was in the line of breakage. A number of chimneys were also knocked down. This was about the total damage in Marked Tree. People were badly frightened and hurriedly left the buildings regardless, in some cases, of appearances. The electric lights at Lepanto, twelve miles away, were knocked out of commission.

A second tremor came late in the afternoon of November 26. It was similar to the first one, but did not last so long. I was coming home from Marked Tree in the wagon and had stopped to fix a tangled bridle, standing directly in front of the team when the rumbling began. Fortunately for me, Sam and Rhody had learned to take the shocks and roars of life philosophically. They remained calm, even though the noise was intensified by the rustling of dry leaves along the slough. The ducks and cats — the only other animals on the farm at that time — were less tranquil about the whole thing. They were still quacking and howling when I got home. Maybe hungry.

Most of the human inhabitants of the region followed the mules' example and showed no noticeable concern over the earthquakes. The shocks seemed to have affected the morale of only a few poor ignorant Negroes and a smattering of fanatics, some of whom immediately set to work making horrible predictions about the end of the world, showing a marked resemblance, I thought, to our ducks and cats.

Perhaps I shouldn't make too light of those benighted souls who saw in the seismic shocks a sign of impending doom. Maybe they knew something we didn't, for our fate was shortly sealed — not by an earthquake, however, but by a torch from Prometheus.

Will was in town at the time, and Mr. Keth and I were alone that fateful Sunday morning in early February, 1924. Although I wasn't feeling well, I had gotten up and dressed, then took my boots off and stretched out in the front room while Mr. Keth puttered around in the kitchen, cleaning up after breakfast and brushing his false teeth. I was almost asleep when I heard him yelling. Dimly the words took shape in my sleep-clouded mind: "Roy! The house is on fire!" Leaping up in my stocking feet, I saw him running to the stairs, where dense smoke was billowing down. We grabbed up several buckets of water and rushed up through the smoke, only to find the whole second story ablaze. The water we threw on the flames was slightly less effective than

137

the proverbial snowball in Hades. We tried in vain to reach a trunk containing valuable papers and other items, finally retreating with only a small box of worthless odds and ends.

Downstairs we salvaged a few things — some bedding, meat, and a small table from the front room, which Mr. Keth carried out so carefully that none of the small articles on it were disturbed (one of them was *The Handbook of Recipes,* which remains in the family after all these years). Mr. Keth also managed to save his and Will's shotguns, his own suitcase, and a few other bits and pieces.

One of the more serious losses was that of Mr. Keth's false teeth, which he had been cleaning when he first saw the flames. In his excitement he'd forgotten to put them back into his mouth. Yet he regained enough composure to carry the table out delicately.

Except for some "Sunday-go-to-meetin' " clothes we kept at a friend's room in town, we lost all our clothing, including my boots and all but one sock (I'd been wearing both when the fire started but one of them got lost in the shuffle).

Relatively high winds at the time probably accounted for the rapid spread of the fire and prevented us from hearing the flames sooner. We never knew how it started — probably from a hot spark on the roof or a defective flue. Luckily, we had removed several hundred pounds of cotton from the house just a week before it burned.

As Mr. Keth and I stood around dumbfoundedly staring at the charred remains of our house, Mr. Robinson, from Dr. Baird's farm, showed up to commiserate with us. Soon he began to probe in the hot embers and eventually located a large ham, which he took with him when he left. We spent that night and a few days afterward at Haversticks', then later stayed awhile with the Robinsons, where we got part of the ham back in the meals we ate with them. Under the blackened outside, it had been cooked to perfection by the holocaust.

It was a dreary time for Will and me. After doing clear-

138

ing work for several years, we were still in the woods worse than ever. This final fire of tribulation had caused us searing spiritual pain. It seemed that the only trail in the wilderness left for us was the one leading out of it. It is trite but true to say that we were live actors in life's tragedy, confronted with the annual threat of flood waters swirling about us, with boll weevils gouging at every cotton boll, with our own dwelling in smouldering ruins and our other houses untenanted with no prospects of filling them; and so we felt that it might be better to retreat in tatters now, and reappear a little better garbed later, the Lord willing.

More or less out of desperation, we turned over the operation of the farm to a neighbor, Lonnie Lane. Later we learned that he was more interested in moonshining than in farming and had apparently rented the place with an eye on the Broadmouth woods, which offered ideal cover for illicit stills.

I made plans to return to Ohio. Will clerked for a time at the Arkansaw Drug Store in Marked Tree, then went back to his old job of lumber inspector.

Throughout most of 1924, I worked in Ohio, helping my father with farm work on our home place that winter and into the spring of the following year. In August, 1925, I set out on an expedition through the South — North Carolina, Tennessee, and northern Alabama — that ultimately led me back to Arkansas in October. The farm had been rented that year to our good neighbor, John Haverstick, who had living on it, as a sharecropper, a widow named Ola Emmons. Unusual as it was, she seemed every bit as capable as a man, and had managed to work her crop while taking good care of her three small children. I helped with the cotton picking on our place, and when that was finished, resumed my long-delayed efforts at clearing more of our land. It was while I was thus engaged on the business end of a forester's axe that my next, and last, great Arkansas adventure began.

XIV GOLDEN RULE DAYS:

Tenting on the Old Schoolground

Many noble sentiments have been expressed about the teaching profession, but I've always liked what Lord Chesterfield said: "The vanity of teaching doth tempt a man to forget he is a blockhead." I suspect that has some application to my own meager efforts to light a candle of understanding in young minds. With me, school teaching in Arkansas might well have been characterized by Dr. Johnson's famous remark about women preachers: the miracle was not that it was done well, but that it was done at all.

In 1922 Arkansas ranked forty-sixth among the states in expenditures for education, and our own county of Crittenden held the dubious honor of having the highest illiteracy rate of any county in the state. That same year there were two bright youngsters of school age living on our place and any number of others on surrounding farms, yet the only school was more than five miles away. Barely half of this distance was covered by a newly-cut, undrained, muddy road. Over the other half there was no road at all, hardly even a

140

trail through the boggy woods. Thus it was out of the question for the children to attend classes. During all our first four and a half years on the farm — until 1923 — none of the children there nor those on the Baird or Haverstick farms adjoining us had ever attended school. This represented at least thirty or forty families over the years. All were simply too far in the woods to be within access of a school for either white or black children.

Conditions had improved very little by late 1925, when I returned to the farm. A small one-room building — known as Broadmouth School — had been erected about two miles northeast of our farm, near Luttrell's Landing, but it offered only the most remote resemblance to an educational institution. In one or two previous school years, classes had been held there sporadically through perhaps two four-month terms, but there had been constant problems in keeping teachers, maintaining discipline, and getting the children to attend regularly. The school had a reputation as being tough on teachers; apparently the last two had been completely unable to control their charges and had given up in disgust.

By December, 1925, I had been working by myself for a month or so, doing clearing work, "treading the winepress alone," as Isaiah says. I was swinging the axe as usual one day when Bob Sims, who lived on the fine Cummins farm some two miles north of us, came riding up on a mule and asked if I would be interested in teaching school at Broadmouth. I had taught one year back in Ohio almost a decade earlier, but I don't think Bob knew that then, if ever. He said nothing about previous experience, nor did he even mention a teaching certificate, which in fact I did not have at that time. Perhaps he knew I had gone to college; at any rate, I read a lot and talked like a Yankee and had been clean to Asheville, N.C. I suppose that was recommendation enough.

I told Bob I'd think it over and let him know. To find out what teaching in the boondocks might be like, I went almost halfway to Marked Tree to visit a country school in progress. I had misgivings about being able to handle some of the wild offspring I'd encountered, but the young school-marm where I visited seemed to have things under control. If she could do it, so could I.

I talked to a county school official in Marked Tree and worked out the arrangements. There was to be a four-month term starting about the first of the year, with perhaps two more months after crops were laid by in the summer and before the harvest season would begin. My salary was set at eighty-five dollars a month.

Next, I went to inspect the hall of learning over which I was to preside. The unpainted frame building, about forty feet long by thirty feet wide, was relatively new and in good condition despite its use during off seasons as a barn for storing hay and cotton. School officials bought some stovepipe for the wood-burning stove, and I connected it to the chimney. The blackboard was too small, so I bought some wallboard and painted it black. It seemed to serve quite well. There was a tiny table for the teacher, but nothing to sit on, so I bought myself a chair. Expenses for such incidentals came out of my pocket.

According to the *Biographical and Historical Memoirs of Northeast Arkansas,* compiled in 1889, there were by 1886 a number of new schools in the Marked Tree area, all of which were "well furnished, with patent seats, blackboards, and other necessary apparatus." Obviously, things had not gone well in the ensuing forty years. Broadmouth School had no desks whatever, only long benches, about thirteen altogether, each accommodating five pupils. A quarter-century later, on a visit to the British Isles in 1950, I sat in a seat in the oldest schoolroom in continuous use in England — one at Eton College for Boys, in use since 1440. Here there had been desks all through the centuries. They were narrow and much initialed, but this five-century-old school was more modern in that respect than the one in which I taught in Arkansas. In fact, most rural schools in

142

this country a century earlier were better equipped than Broadmouth School. Horace Mann, writing in 1838, reported that "seats and desks (in country school houses) are sometimes designed only for a single scholar and allow the teacher to approach on either side, and give an opportunity to go out or into the seat, without disturbance of anyone."

The lack of desks at Broadmouth not only caused such disturbances but also created the more serious problem of requiring each child to hold his book in his hands or lap when studying and to write with his paper resting only on a book before him in his lap. Nor was any special place provided for books, lunch baskets, hats, or coats. We had no bell except a tiny dinner gong, which I rang with considerable vigor to make up for its diminutive tinkle. A single water bucket and chipped porcelain dipper served all comers, although we had a driven well nearby to supply fresh drinking water (like all local water supplies, it provided "running water" — the kind you ran out and got). All my students took their books home each evening — not so much for study, I'm afraid, as to prevent anything happening to them. Everyone was guardian over his own property.

For awhile after the term began, and despite a bad cold, I walked the two miles to school from our farm each day, usually accompanied by two of my pupils, Mrs. Emmons' little girl and boy, Virgie, nine, and Olin, seven. To get to school, we walked along an old tramroad on which a tram had been used many years before to transport logs up to Luttrell's Landing.

Then, after a couple of weeks, it became apparent that the trip was too difficult for the little Emmons children, so John Haverstick (for whom Mrs. Emmons was sharecropping on our place) suggested that the family take one of his big logger tents up near the north end of the tramway only a few hundred feet from the schoolhouse. He helped them set it up, and there was so much room that John and Mrs. Emmons suggested that I might find it more convenient to stay there too. And that is how I came to live with a widow and three children in a tent in the wilderness.

Perhaps it was a bit unorthodox, but it sounds more sensational than it really was. I paid a dollar a day for board and lodging, and my section of the tent was divided off by blankets and quilts, leaving only a small open space where I could get heat from the wood stove when grading papers and preparing lessons. Yet it was quite comfortable and homey. Apparently none of the neighbors thought anything of the arrangement, and not an eyebrow was lifted. (If it seems odd to suggest that anyone would object to my living with the widow, in view of all the killing, moonshining, and random bedding I've described, I should add that while the local moral code allowed for all kinds of straying, it put forth a rigidly Puritanical attitude that few dared flaunt openly. Apparently I was considered harmless, as indeed I was.)

In a letter home I wrote that "Mrs. Emmons moved her chickens with her (from our farm) and we have plenty of eggs. The hens are accommodating and lay eggs in the tent everyday."

The total number of white children of school age in the Broadmouth district was said to be 105, but the number enrolled under me was only sixty-three, and average attendance rarely went over forty, for many attended just a week or two. (Negro children attended school — in a somewhat more substantial building — several miles away on the Black Oak Road.)

The plan had been to hold classes for grades one through seven, but none of my pupils had gone beyond the sixth grade. Almost all of them were much behind for their ages. The oldest student was seventeen and in the fifth grade. The average age for the primer class was eight or nine years. According to the register of ages kept by the previous teacher, the average age of pupils then in the second grade was 11.4 years. My oldest second-grader, Zella Finley, was fourteen and engaged to be married. Several weeks after

144

school started, a ten-year-old boy came to school for the first time in his life, and a few days later his twelve-year-old brother made his initial appearance. They could scarcely keep up with the primer class, which had had only a slight head start. And there were about forty in the district who never showed up at all. Dropouts troubled me less than those who never bothered to drop in.

I doubt that there was one pupil in the school who could have done the work expected of students his age in most other schools. Few of the pupils of ten or twelve or even fourteen were able to tell time, and when school began hardly any could have named a half-dozen states. Hopefully, I felled a few logs in that forest of ignorance. It was certainly dense enough.

They seemed almost as backward on the playground as in the schoolroom. Chasing each other around seemed to be the main diversion. Looking back, I regret that I did not take more interest in their playground activities and in showing them games to play, for surely that sort of instruction would have been as vital and meaningful to them as the things they got from books. At the time, I considered it something of a miracle that I was able merely to keep the peace and that there were so few fights on the schoolground. The scarcity of rocks in the region removed one common danger to windows and youthful noggins.

One of the first things the children had learned to spell, if anything, was their names, and the results were interesting, if sometimes quite sad. A boy in the third grade, Horace, spelled his name "Hairce." Arthur spelled his "Arther," and Ophelia — she was twelve and in the second grade — spelled hers "Ofilger." Her older sister, who was fifteen and in the third grade, told me that the last teacher had spelled it the way I did, so since two teachers had agreed upon the same spelling, the family would spell it that way (although a third teacher had apparently had still a different spelling for it).

"Hairce" and "Arther," however, remained steadfast and

refused to accept any arbitration, stoutly maintaining that their spelling was correct. I had no better luck with another boy, whose name sounded like the girl's name "Bernice," but who insisted on spelling it "Burnice."

All through that winter we endured health conditions that by any other standards were abominable. For the first several weeks, I was plagued with a terrible cold that I couldn't seem to shake off. Walking several miles to school in chilly, damp weather and frequently having to gather stovewood in driving rains no doubt contributed to my condition, which for a time threatened to turn into pneumonia. But no one thought much of a simple cold — the children sniffed constantly, and many of them came to school afflicted with malaria, chills, chicken pox, and head lice.

Lice, like colds, were more or less taken for granted. The kids often quoted the old saw, "Adam had 'em, Eve had 'em, and we have 'em, too." Frequently I noticed the girls in pairs, one of them sitting down, the other standing behind her conducting a search through the first girl's hair. I learned that the mother of one boy had once found ten lice and a number of mites on his head. But the record delousing at school was sixteen, picked from a girl's head by several others one noon. Louse-picking was primarily a female concern; I don't think the boys ever paid much attention to the pestiferous little insects.

Somehow I managed to stay free of lice, although it was reported that previous teachers had been afflicted with them. "Ever'body was lousy last year," said a small girl earnestly. A rumor got out that I had said Broadmouth was the lousiest school I had ever taught, and I was reproached by some of the older girls for my apparent lack of loyalty. I don't believe I ever uttered such a statement, at least not audibly.

An incident concerning lice illustrates the type of ignorance and superstition that confronted me as a teacher. A boy in a neighbor's home once handed me a head louse, and when I suggested putting it in the stove, the old grandmother called out, "Don't! If you do, nine more will come in its place!" And I faced a common superstition when, in history class, the subject of witchcraft came up, several girls insisted that witches and warlocks were real, bolstering their arguments with "examples."

Discipline was of course the most immediate problem I faced, for instruction of any kind can hardly take place amid turmoil and confusion. I was reminded of the fellow who set out to show a friend how to train a mule. His first act was to pick up a two-by-four and crack the mule between the ears, almost knocking the animal off its feet. "Why'd you do that?" said the astonished friend. "Well," said the fellow, "first you've got to get his attention."

There were indications that the same was true of rowdy country kids. One of the larger boys bore a big scar on his cheek, where a previous teacher had landed on him with a stick, probably in self-defense. I must admit, however, that I had expected more trouble than I actually encountered.

One means of preventing disorder was to segregate the sexes, putting the girls on benches to the teacher's left, and boys on those to the right. There were, as I recall, seven rows on the boys' side and six on the girls', with the water bucket, stove and woodpile occupying a space on the girls' side where one seat would otherwise have been.

One of my late-comers was a rather large boy whose bad reputation had preceded him. I felt his case called for drastic preventive action and decided to break custom by putting him in a front seat on the girls' side. It worked only too well — he was so humiliated that he dropped out after a few days, telling another pupil, "I can't have any fun in school." I regretted it, but leniency was a luxury I could rarely afford.

Under such primitive conditions, one has to be strict and keep things under control, yet at the same time try to be fair and pleasant. There was also the danger of stirring up parental enmity, too, for the more backward parents were likely to stand up for their children regardless of circumstances — and, as I've made clear, a gun was frequently

147

the arbiter in local disputes. Within six months after I returned to Arkansas in 1925, there were three killings within two miles of us, as well as several attempts to dynamite drainage levees in a tough community just across the river. Teaching was real missionary work.

I did not keep track of just how many lickings I administered. There were not many, and I trust that all of them were justifiable. In one corner at the front of the room I kept a pecan switch in plain sight. That was my "birching block." It would disappear from time to time, but there were lots of pecan sprouts nearby, so I would simply cut another.

Soon after the school term opened, several children warned me about one particular troublemaker — an older girl — who had given previous teachers much anguish. She turned out to be the daughter of Bob Sims, the fellow originally responsible for my taking the teaching job. Bessie was a big, strong girl of about fifteen and, in the manner of a stout Teutonic maiden, rather attractive. For some reason or another, she did not start at the beginning of the term, but when she finally showed up after a few days, she was soon in the center of a commotion in the back of the room. I called a halt, and made Bessie face the blackboard at the front of the room, and measured the height of her nose on the board. Then I drew a small circle just a trifle higher, and told her to put her nose in it. "Every time you take your nose out of the ring, you'll stand here five minutes longer," I told her. Since nothing had been indicated as to how long this would be anyway, I had plenty of leeway.

I looked up occasionally to check on her nose . . . and to see how well she was bearing up. She took it stoically for almost forty minutes, but then I saw a tear or two and, aware that she was beginning to tire, I let her take her seat. Without resorting to any real physical pain, I had inflicted pretty severe punishment. Although it didn't completely subdue Bessie, she was much more manageable after that.

148

Moreover, I seemed to have gained her respect, and we got along quite well.

However, I made a mistake in letting her keep her seat in the back. One day I detected a ground swell of snickers in the room. The cause was not difficult to spot. In fact, there were a good many spots — where Bessie had marked up her face with crayons of various colors. She would have attracted attention even among wild Samoan tribesmen. "Come up front," I ordered. She came, carrying a book. "Now," I said, "turn around so everyone can see how pretty you look." She turned around, but held up the book before her face. It was no longer so funny, and she soon returned to her seat in humiliation.

With the lid clamped on her classroom antics, Bessie took out her frustrations on some of the smaller children when they were away from the schoolground. Two of those who seemed to suffer most were a girl named Thelma Sharp and her little brother, R. M. The Sharp children, who were quiet, well-behaved youngsters, constantly complained that Bessie hit and bullied them as they walked home after school. I spoke to Bessie about it (which of course was wasted breath), but assumed that my jurisdiction went no further. I was to learn, authoritatively, that the teacher's responsibility lasted until pupils reached home.

The situation worsened rapidly, and for a time it seemed that the parents might literally take up arms. Several of them expressed their concern in letters to me (all of which I saved, interested not so much at the time in their color-ful expressions as in protecting myself with the school board). One note came from the father of the Sharp children; another was from the mother of Andrew Asbury, who complained that her son, too, was being "jomped on" by the Sims girl. Mrs. Asbury wrote in part:

> Mr. Roy will rite you a few lines. Regards of my little boy yesterday evning there was 3 of Mr. Sims kids all jomped on him and Bessie is to big to jomp on a

12 year boy. I have whiped him for fighting my last time. . . . My boy has no got no Brother or sister or father to take his part. . . . She got mad becose Andrew taken up for the little Sharp girl it is this way evry school I have whiped him for fighting on the road home and now I am going to whip him if he dont take his Part from now on. . . . I want Andrew to mind you. I teach him to do so. Yours truly . . .

Thelma Sharp wrote some lines to Bessie which I happened to intercept. They concluded: "I dont want you to start anything this evning but I am not scared of you I no that you and Bernice can whelp me and R. M."

The letter to me from Mr. Sharp was simply a brief note showing no hostility at all, asking if I would please let his children out of school ahead of Bessie Sims because there might be trouble if she continued to bother them. Taking the hint, I let Thelma and R. M. leave fifteen minutes before classes usually ended. The minute the others were released, Bessie took off in a gallop, trying to overtake them. Apparently she failed, and I concluded that that was the solution to the problem.

But Bessie's presence — or as the case may be, the lack of it — continued to create excitement. One afternoon just after school was out, a logger drove up to the school with a wagon and team and asked for Bessie. I suppose he wanted to ask her for a date, but I never found out. When he learned that she was already on her way home, he ran out and unhooked the left wheel mule (always used for riding) from the four-up hitch, jumped on it, and galloped away at top speed, leaving the other three mules standing by the schoolhouse door. I learned later that he didn't find her; apparently even a mule couldn't overtake Bessie when she was in her stride.

On another occasion, I discovered on a wall of the boys' outhouse some obscene phrases containing the name of this

150

same young lady who was so frequently in the thick of things. The words had been printed rather than written. No reflection was cast on anyone, and it wasn't of vital importance that the miscreant be ferreted out. Moreover, I knew it would be futile to inquire openly. But my curiosity was aroused, and I hit upon a stealthy plan to discover the toilet Tennyson. Part of every Friday afternoon I devoted to a respite from regular school work, devising various programs involving recitations, readings, and spelling contests. The winners were awarded small prizes that I bought from time to time at a variety store in town. This was a big event for most of those poor kids, and occasionally even a parent or two would show up. I'm sure I looked forward to it as much as they did.

On one of these Friday afternoons, I tried out my plan to reveal the identity of Bessie's outhouse biographer. In the program I included for the whole school some practice writing and an exercise in printing, with emphasis on the same letters I had observed—in a different arrangement, of course. Then I gathered the papers as if to grade them, and later compared them with a copy I had carefully made of the mystery printing. The only thing I learned was that everyone prints alike. If the original letters had been written out, there might have been some chance of identification, but as it was, the experiment convinced me that I was no cryptographer, and to this day, the Case of the Broadmouth School Boys' Outhouse Scribbler remains unsolved.

With so little else in the way of diversion, the kids turned to affairs of the heart, often at remarkably tender ages. Fervid romances, intrigues, and eternal triangles flourished in a storm of guileful flirtations, note passing, initial carving, and, ultimately, broken hearts (which usually healed with the passing of time — perhaps a day or two).

An eleven-year-old boy was an ardent wooer of a girl of eight, but some trouble came between them. At noon one day she sent an intermediary to tell him she was quitting him — "he has used me like a dog." When her lover got the word, he put his head in his hands and cried and cried as though his heart would break. "She won't find another fellow who will stand up for her like I have," he asserted, alluding to the previous summer, when he had fought another boy in her behalf. He was so upset he missed his spelling lesson, and I kept him after school to get it. To the surprise of both of us, the little girl waited to walk home with him.

But "the course of true love runs not smooth," and before long they had another spat. Then, during classes one day, she carried a book to him and whispered for him to look inside. My suspicions aroused, I confiscated the book and intercepted the note, which I kept and have before me as I write, one of my treasured possessions. It bears no salutation, but goes directly and succinctly to the heart of the matter: "I love you. If you will not get mad at me any more. So good by. Alice."

Although Alice was only eight years old, she was in the fourth grade, and was perhaps the brightest youngster in school. Thus it was a great shock when at recess one day she suddenly began to scream and cry. Then I noticed that she was pointing toward her home, only a short distance from the school. It was a mass of flames. Ordering the children to stay back, I rushed over, but soon saw that the fire had engulfed the entire building. Alice's father was standing in the yard, in such a state of shock as to be helpless. It was impossible to get inside, but I managed to grab a wagon seat off the porch, and that much at least was saved. The family was fortunate in finding another house in the area. It was much farther from school, but still close enough that Alice could attend classes.

But back to the subject of young love. From time to time I intercepted other romantic missives, usually from girls to their sweethearts. One of them reads: "I have something to tell you. I hope it isn't so for I love you as well as I ever will. But you don't me do you? BBS." A second one is more heartwarming: "Dearest sweetie I love

152

you better than I do Lonnie. Can I beat Bessie Sims time I
hope I can. I will close."

Other of my treasures from those lost golden days
include several sheets of verses copied by one boy among
my charges. The fumbling phrases and almost undecipher-
able scrawl are redeemed by the sad intensity of:

> It is sweet to meet
> But oh how bitter
> To love a girl
> And then cant get her

Other samples:

> The sea is wide and sometimes muddy
> Your blue eyes is all I study

> —

> The roads are long and lonesome
> The sea is black
> I think of you, little darling
> Ten thousand times a week

> —

> I love pumpkin
> I love squash
> I love you, I do, By Gosh

> —

> And when you get married
> And live on a hill
> Send me a kiss by the
> Whip-poor-will

I ultimately lost three pupils to Cupid before the four-
month school term ended. One of them was my fourteen-
year-old second-grader, Zella Finley. One day at noon she

153

seemed sick and wanted to go home, so I excused her. But apparently her illness was only an act to decoy me and her parents. That night she was married at a garage in Marked Tree by a justice of the peace. (The unusual setting is accounted for by the fact that Squire O'Roark, who married the couple, was an employee of Blanton's Garage, in addition to his duties as justice of the peace. Large numbers of local couples set out on the road of matrimony from Blanton's.) At the time of her marriage, Zella had just turned fifteen, and I had promoted her to the third grade as a birthday present. Another girl, slightly older, was well along in a family way before quitting school to get married.

When the initial term ended in April, 1926, it seemed that my work had hardly begun. But book learning had to be set aside, for it was planting time, and the children were needed in the fields. Although our farm was now rented to Dr. Baird, I busied myself with numerous tasks about the place, largely that of clearing more land, assisted now and then by our old dependable helper, Mr. Keth. Dr. Baird's overseer, Siah Morris, moved into our remaining house on Broadmouth, and I stayed there most of the time while working on the farm. Mr. Morris was, like Mr. Keth, an agreeable bachelor, and a good cook to boot.

We had planned — or hoped — to have two more months of school after laying-by time in the summer, but apparently the school district's meager funds played out. I heard one day that the benches, stove, and other furnishings were being cleared out of the school building to convert it back to a barn for crop storage. I arrived just in time to salvage my teacher's chair, which I had paid for myself.

So ended the saga of Broadmouth School. What transpired there in later years I cannot say, for shortly afterward I again said goodbye to the delta lowlands of Arkansas — this time, as it turned out, for good.

I'm not foolhardy enough to venture any brash observa-

154

tions on what may have been accomplished during my brief tenure as schoolmaster in the backwoods. Sometimes it seemed quite futile, as when I once spent more than a week trying to teach my second-grade arithmetic class how to tell time. And I suspect that more than half of them never quite grasped the significant distinction between the "big hand" and the "little hand."

But there were other times, when a distant gleam came to the eye of a sharecropper's shaggy-headed son, and a little girl ran home to tell her mama about Gibraltar and New York, exotic places where monkeys scampered down matted slopes and people rode great motor cars in the deep canyons of marble and steel. There was the time a gawky fourteen-year-old finally grasped the meaning of "put down two and carry one," and the time little Alice Corrigan proudly reported that she had read "clean through" her fourth-grade reader. I take some comfort in the words of Anatole France, who said, "The whole art of teaching is only the art of awakening the natural curiosity of young minds for the purpose of satisfying it afterwards." If that's true — and I think it is — I did my job.

Rewards came in other ways, too. Only a few years before Broadmouth School was built, those who wanted to cross the slough up near Luttrell's had to make their way gingerly over on a rough log. Now, because most of my pupils lived across the slough from the schoolhouse, a primitive bridge had been built for their convenience. This, too, was progress — progress that the little muddy-trail newcomers could not appreciate, nor share with me. And what changes have taken place since then! Now a bus takes the youngsters to school in town, and hopefully those old, hard days I have described are gone forever. But what rich memories they call to mind . . .

XV THE TRAIL ENDS:

Of Time, the River, and the Men

"Men and marked trees come and go. They cannot prevail against 'the tooth of time and razure of oblivion.' " So concluded a writer for *The Arkansas Gazette* in 1926, sadly noting the encroachment of civilization upon our once-remote corner of Arkansas. Apparently the twentieth century was finally reaching Marked Tree. The town square — all three blocks of it — had been paved, and cars were beginning to outnumber cows on Main Street. Several homes in town had radio receivers, and the area's first rural mail delivery service was inaugurated that year. Crude roadways were penetrating the woodlands, a few farmers were experimenting with a new-fangled, steam-propelled implement called the tractor, and there was talk of an extensive flood control program that would keep the delta drained and dry the year 'round. Utopian as all this may have seemed to the *Gazette's* alarmed columnist, however, the region still retained much of its frontier character; the job of civilizing

156

Marked Tree was left to the forty intervening years since he issued his lament.

For Will and me, the changes came almost imperceptibly, despite the sudden jolts that stirred and shifted our lives and changed them in ways we little realized or understood. I suspect it is that way with most people, for no matter how we try to plan our lives and settle the order of things, the slightest whim or bending breeze commits us to another course. Inevitably, "way leads on to way," as Robert Frost so perceptively put it, and the road not taken often guides our steps as surely as the one we tread.

Looking back, I see little plan or purpose in the events that immediately followed our disastrous fire and my abortive career as schoolmaster. If anything, they merely formed a fitting anticlimax to our Arkansas adventure. It was fated to end with neither bang nor whimper, accompanied instead by little more than the ticking of time, the rustle of calendar leaves, a thing simply played out and gradually gone.

After Broadmouth School closed in the spring of 1926, I took up the axe again and went back to clearing more ground on our farm, which we had rented to Dr. Baird that year. It was being farmed by his sharecroppers, with Siah Morris as overseer.

In a month or two we decided to halt clearing operations for the time being, and I "hired out" to John Haverstick, working with him until late summer, when the crops were laid by. Then I heard of an interesting job on a dairy farm in northern Mississippi, just south of Memphis, and John, always accommodating, drove me there to see about it. I little realized then that this was my farewell to Arkansas.

After two years in Mississippi, I was homesick for Ohio (and practically hand-crippled from milking eighteen cows twice a day!) During this period, and for some years after, the farm was usually rented by Dr. Baird, who cared for the land as if it were his own and saw to it that his tenants did not "work it to death" as so many try to do. Will, who had married in the meantime, checked on the farming

157

operations from time to time while continuing his work as a lumber inspector in Arkansas and Louisiana. I sold my interest in the farm to him and headed north to become a Buckeye once again.

The years that followed were pleasant, rewarding ones, but almost uncomfortably tame and phlegmatic compared to the time we struggled in the Arkansas wilderness. In Ohio, through the early years of the Depression, I worked for H. V. Shulters, president of Cleveland's National City Bank, who owned one of the country's finest registered Guernsey herds. After Mr. Shulters' death, I went back to the family farm to work with my father, and shortly afterward married Edna Wilson, whom I had known before going to Arkansas, when we taught school together in Frazeysburg. Following our marriage and the retirement of my father-in-law, I managed his farm, located near Newark, Ohio, not far from my own home area around Zanesville. Meanwhile, in 1935, Will, his wife Gladys, and their two little girls, Bobbye and Donna, settled in Marked Tree, and Will resumed the work of clearing ground on the farm, a job we had begun sixteen years earlier. He toiled all that summer and much of the winter in the low-lying area partly encircled by Little Broadmouth, clearing over ten acres. Yet a large section of nearly forty acres remained in timber until sometime in the 1940's; the complete transformation from forest to farm took almost a quarter of a century.

Other changes came, often just as gradually. By the late 1930's flood control and improved farming practices resulted in crop yields that were phenomenal in comparison with the sorry results we usually experienced in our early years in the area. In 1936, fifty-one acres on our farm produced nearly forty-eight bales of cotton — almost more than the combined total of all our cotton crops in the early twenties. Certainly the per-acre yield was many times anything we had ever dreamed possible.

With the new road now opened up along our south line, the center of activity on the farm shifted from our

158

original homesite up on Big Broadmouth. The one remaining house there fell apart from neglect; mechanization meant that more land could be worked with less labor, and the need for tenant houses diminished. The barn was torn down and some of its lumber used in the construction of a new, more modern one near the houses on the southeastern corner of the farm. Eventually they, too, succumbed to the ravages of time.

What has happened to the town of Marked Tree in the intervening half-century since Will and I first went there is perhaps best described in the words from a poem by Grover Lewis, Texas poet and social critic. "The scene changes but nothing actual changes," he wrote. "Nothing good enough can happen." Marked Tree today is the same town, where, as my niece, who grew up there, puts it, "the kids still steal watermelons for sport, drive cars when they are big enough to peer over the wheel, get their beer from the Negro side of town, marry young and divorce quickly." Yet, inevitably, it has changed too, in the way of a thousand other American small towns, whose natural inclination to drowse along through the twentieth century has been imposed upon by two world wars and a depression, as well as drastically changing social attitudes, hot rods, drive-in movies, bikinis, Batman, electric toothbrushes, civil rights, cybernetics, moon-shots, and hamburger stands with names like Duke's Kream Kan or The Purple Cow.

But of course some things never change. One of the delta's more famous personages is Carroll Cloar, whose forebears helped found and settle the town of Earle, just south of Marked Tree. Today Cloar is an eminent artist who records his boyhood memories of the region in rich and delicate tempera. Of the area he writes, "Summer dies as slowly and stubbornly as ever. But the gravel road is blacktopped now, there are fewer trees and more and more ordered rows of cotton. If you go northward in Arkansas you might see people who stepped out of my mother's album — early American faces, timeless dress and timeless customs. But perhaps they are changing, too — the last of an old America which isn't long for this earth."

And so today, Marked Tree is a curious blend of the past and present. The stately, columned Baptist Church and roomy brick bungalows set on broad, tree-shadowed streets are reminders of an older, calmer time . . . but a few blocks away the mechanized traffic of the Soaring Sixties speeds past a gaudy line of super service stations, a television repair shop, a coin-operated car wash, and an unpainted frame grocery store with a fly-specked screen door and a sign that pleads "OPeN COMe iN." On the north side of town is an attractive new low-cost-housing development, a government-financed project of neat duplexes tastefully designed and landscaped, just a short distance from the riverfront shanties that seem to have been there forever. A scrubby houseboat is moored in exactly the same spot where Will took a picture of it more than forty years ago, and it looks just as it did then, still a patchwork affair of tar paper and lumber scraps. The business district, though not much larger than when we were there, is now neat and substantial, most of the rickety frame buildings having been replaced or remodeled. The town's anachronisms are symbolized by a beautifully-restored 1929 Plymouth parked in a driveway on one of the quiet streets. For an instant, one has the very real sensation that he has gone back four decades — until he sees the television antennas and picture windows, and realizes that the car is not painted the traditional black of its milieu, but is refinished in a delicately garish lemon-lime hue, marking it — and the entire scene — as an imperfect reproduction, out of its time and place.

Back in the twenties, Marked Tree was largely a company town for the Chapman and Dewey Lumber Company. Today, "C & D" has been replaced by Ritter and Company, whose extensive farming, real estate, and utilities interests are administered from the top floor of the massive three-story Ritter Building, a futuristic cube of glass and drab concrete slabs covering almost half a block near the center

160

of town. Among Marked Tree's other business establish-
ments, most of which are quartered in small, single-story
buildings with false fronts still jutting above their modern-
ized facades, the Ritter Building is, to say the least, distinctive. Its ground floor is occupied by a supermarket, and
the second story is deserted except for a lone dentist's office
in one corner.

In contrast to its raw, under-developed nature fifty years
ago, the Marked Tree area today boasts a relatively stable,
prosperous economy, as indicated by some of the illustrious
company it keeps — former President Eisenhower, according
to the *New York Times*, holds some stock in the industrial
future of the town, presented to him by C. A. Dawson,
farm manager for the Ritter concern. Little did we dream
when we invested in Arkansas gumbo back in 1919 that we
might one day be in the company of so prominent a person-
age.

The economy — one based entirely on agriculture — also
shows increasing signs of diversification. One of the more
thriving new industries is a concern that manufactures
blackboards and display materials. A booming business is
also being done in mussel shells (used in making buttons)
dredged from the bottom of the Little River north of town.

On U.S. Route 63 just east of the city limits and not
far from where the Black Oak Road stretches south toward
our farm, there is a lavish new Travelair Motel, replete
with swimming pool, television, air conditioning, a Courtesy-
Coffee machine in every room, and an ebullient clerk who
promises you "the best lil ole room yore tokus was ever in."

The Black Oak Road is paved now, and the trip from
town out to the farm that once took us at least half a day
even when the weather was good can now be made in about
ten minutes, without breaking any speed laws. Across the
road from where Black Oak School once stood is a modern
cinder-block grocery store and service station that sells
everything from plug tobacco to paper towels behind a
brick-and-glass front plastered with the inevitable tin signs

161

proclaiming the virtues of Dr. Pepper, Doan's Pills, Robin Hood Flour, and Grove's Chill Tonic. Such an establishment would truly have been an oasis to us back in the twenties. Two miles further south is a graveled, all-weather road — the one my brother helped build — that runs east to the farm. Alongside it are the "high-line" poles of a local rural electric co-operative.

The area bears little resemblance to the isolated woodland where we settled forty-seven years ago. Gone are the vast stands of timber that closed us in, and the flat land lies dark and bald across great open plats of the delta plain, dotted with only an occasional ridge of oak or ash, like wisps of fur on a moth-eaten pelt. Gone too are most of the traces of our pioneering venture: all the original buildings, the log dump, the foot paths and wagon trails. Where we once paddled a johnboat and rafted logs through Broadmouth Flats, today a car can cross the dry slough bed on a wide earthen bridge and drive over improved roadway that was once a rutted, stump-dotted trail, beside which stood the Haverstick home, commissary, and tenant houses. No vestige of them remains. And although the original homesteads on older places like that of ours and Haversticks' have disappeared, the surrounding farms, cleared out more recently in the late thirties and forties, are heavily clustered with houses and outbuildings, some of them already deserted in the wake of mechanization and declining farm prices, but others are surrounded by bright new cars and bedecked with television antennas and air conditioners and aluminum awnings. They house farm workers rather than land owners (most of whom have moved into town), but the buildings, with their fresh coats of paint and neat yards, are a far cry from the tenant houses — or even the boss-man's home — in our time.

Broadmouth School has vanished — even the name is forgotten — and Luttrell's Landing survives only as dim words in the minds of a new generation ("I bleve I've heard 'em say it was right along yonder, by where that sand

162

bar is now") to whom packet boats and river barges are ghosts of a misty, faded era. Of the landmarks we knew, only the slough and the river remain — and so much of Big Broadmouth has been cleared and filled and leveled that it is hardly recognizable. The St. Francis flows on, deep and gentle between tree-rimmed banks, and its waters are as muddy as ever. But floods are largely a thing of the past, thanks to an extensive system of drainage ditches. Today the trail to Marked Tree is gravel and asphalt, traversed by farmers in two-tone pickup trucks and country boys hitch-hiking into town to look for summer work at the chalkboard factory.

When civilization finally came to Marked Tree, it came quickly. The days of logging camps and new-ground plows and moonshiners and Main Street shoot-outs have been gone for some time, and the things that replaced them have for the most part been good ones. There's much to be said for law and order and electricity and the Rotary Club and Little League baseball and a dozen other aspects of civilization that have settled over Marked Tree. It's a good town, and its citizens have a lot to be proud of.

But every old timer has a license — if not, indeed, an obligation — to call back the past and boost The Good Old Days, and I trust I'll be forgiven if I find too much sound and fury in the world today and long for a gone time when the houses were farther apart and the people closer together. I don't know if life was any better half a century ago when Will and I pioneered in the Arkansas woods — in many ways, of course, it was worse. Surely we did not find Nature as sublime as Thoreau when he took to the woods many decades earlier, yet I applaud some of the philosophical observations for which he, unlike ourselves, had ample time—and ability — to give expression. "I have," he said, "my own sun, and moon, and stars, and a little world all to myself. . . . I would rather sit on a pumpkin and have it all to myself, than to be crowded on a velvet cushion." Of course Henry David lived in his shanty at Walden Pond only two years, and

163

Concord and his mother's apple pies were just a couple of miles away down the Fitchburg Railroad tracks that ran past his retreat; if he had lived in a real wilderness for over twice as long, he might have been a bit less enthusiastic about it. Still, the conditions of backwoods existence imposed an order and meaning upon life that seems missing today. As William H. Milburn wrote in *Ten Years of Preacher Life*, "The terms of tuition in Brush College and Swamp University are high, the course of study hard, but the schooling is capital." What we learned from the rigors and splendors of frontier life is as difficult to explain as it is to evaluate — it has something to do with self-pride and dignity and satisfaction, with lending a man your last dollar at no interest and taking his word that he'll pay it back, with nodding to strangers on the street and leaving your doors unlocked, with thinking your own thoughts and keeping up with yourself instead of the Joneses. Whatever it is, it has stood me in good stead on my travels over the world, to Europe and the Mediterranean, to New Zealand, Australia, and Japan, and although there's much to admire in every culture, I've found nothing for which I'd swap my experiences in the backwoods of Arkansas.

Yet change is of course inevitable, and wishing for a return of the past is a worthless way to occupy oneself. I am content to cherish my years of youthful enterprise in Arkansas not as a standard by which to measure the present, but as an adventure that came and went, leaving me with a deepened perspective that has touched and altered all the years of my life. Out of it comes a thousand flickering spectacles and sensations up the sloping bank of consciousness: the whole vast panorama of twilight-shadowed time, the night-silent woodlands and yellow glow in the window of a tenant shack, the sharp, heavy sweetness of citronella, the firm shock of an axe driven straight and clean into a great oak, the taste and feel and smell of watermelon eaten in the field on summer days . . . the way you instinctively breathe deep to catch the heavy smell of wet earth opened by the plow . . . okra fried in flour, and sweet steaming coffee . . . the monotony of steady rain in wet-haunted winters, and the summertime stench of stagnant backwater pools . . . the pride we took in plowing a straight row through root-tangled new ground . . . the excitement of Saturdays in town, and the bleakness that descended when they were over. And the men, all of them common mortals, yet giants on the earth, who in doing what they had to do, built their own monuments in the wood they cut and the furrows they plowed: George Keth and John Haverstick and Dr. Baird and my brother Will and a hundred like them who led the way and now sleep their long sleeps beneath gentle mounds of the land that is their legacy. Like the marked tree, they have come and gone, on the long, liquid trail of time.

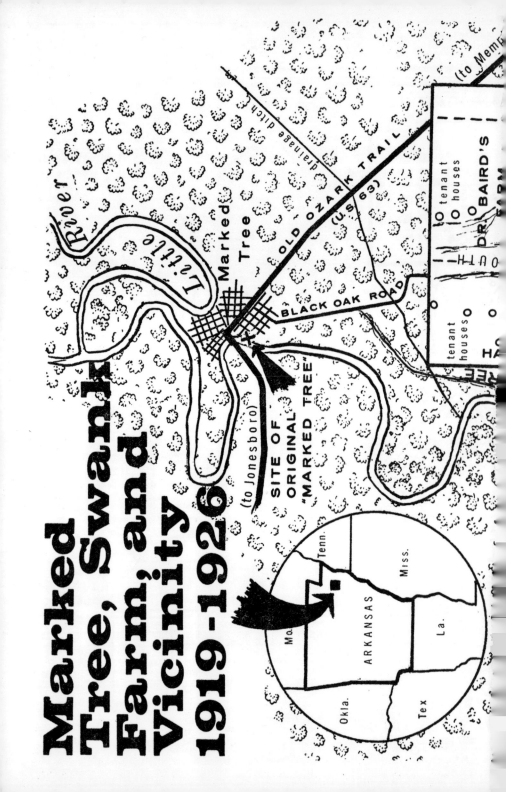

Marked Tree, Swank Farm, and Vicinity 1919-1926

Little River

Marked Tree

drainage ditch

OLD OZARK TRAIL

(U.S. 63)

(to Memp—

BLACK OAK ROAD

tenant houses

DR. BAIRD'S FARM

OUTH

tenant houses

HA—

(to Jonesboro)

SITE OF ORIGINAL "MARKED TREE"

Mo.

Tenn.

Miss.

ARKANSAS

La.

Okla.

Tex